Crisis and Recovery in Malaysia

AF698267

IN MEMORY OF MY MOTHER

Crisis and Recovery in Malaysia

The Role of Capital Controls

Prema-chandra Athukorala

Professor of Economics,
Research School of Pacific and Asian Studies,
Australian National University

Edward Elgar
Cheltenham, UK • Northampton, MA, USA

© Prema-chandra Athukorala 2001

All rights reserved. No part of this publication may be reproduced, stored in a retrieval system or transmitted in any form or by any means, electronic, mechanical or photocopying, recording, or otherwise without the prior permission of the publisher.

Published by
Edward Elgar Publishing Limited
Glensanda House
Montpellier Parade
Cheltenham
Glos GL50 1UA
UK

Edward Elgar Publishing, Inc.
136 West Street
Suite 202
Northampton
Massachusetts 01060
USA

Paperback edition 2003

A catalogue record for this book
is available from the British Library

Library of Congress Cataloguing in Publication Data
Athukorala, Premachandra.
Crisis and recovery in Malaysia : the role of capital control / Prema-chandra Athukorala.
p. cm.
Includes bibliographical references and index.
1. Capital movements—Government policy—Malaysia. 2. Financial crises—Malaysia. 3. Malaysia—Economic policy. 4. Malaysia—Economic conditions. I. Title.
HG3973.6 .A87 2001 00-067342
332'.042—dc21

ISBN 1 84064 621 7 (cased)
1 84376 455 5 (paperback)

Typeset by Manton Typesetters, Louth, Lincolnshire, UK.
Printed and bound in Great Britain by MPG Books Ltd, Bodmin, Cornwall.

Contents

Tables

Figures

Preface

Every major economic crisis stimulates rethinking of fundamental paradigms in economics. A key focus of the 'brainstorming' triggered by the Asian financial crisis of 1997–98 has been on the role of international capital mobility in making countries susceptible to crises and the rationale behind the use of capital controls as a crisis management tool.

This study seeks to contribute to this debate by examining the Malaysian experience through the crisis. Malaysia provides an interesting case study of this subject given its significant capital market liberalization prior to the onset of the crisis, and its bold move in September 1998 to break with the ideological consensus in crisis management that has governed international financial relations over much of the postwar period. Everyone is watching whether Malaysia's radical policy decision to pursue an independent recovery path, cut off from world capital markets by a system of capital controls, would prove to be a viable alternative to the conventional market-centred approach to crisis management.

My original intention was to write a short monograph focusing specifically on the economic implications of capital controls in Malaysia. However, as research progressed I became aware that it was difficult to do justice to the issues at hand without extending the analysis to cover capital account liberalization in the early 1990s and appropriately placing the two episodes in the context of the postwar economic history of Malaysia as well as the experiences of the other East Asian countries through the crisis. Thus the final product turned out to be a sizeable volume dealing with macroeconomic management in Malaysia during the post-independence era, with emphasis on the role of capital control from a comparative East Asian perspective. I hope the volume will be of interest to a wider readership, including development macroeconomists, students of Malaysian and East Asian development, and specialized readers in the area of financial crisis.

I wrote this book conscious of the highly controversial nature of the subject at hand. I have, therefore, been at great pains to be consistently on my guard to include in the book all statistical material and sources of information in order to facilitate scrutiny of my inferences. I have also taken care not to get into the messy debate on the morality of political events surrounding shifts in crisis management policy in Malaysia. Economics is not a morality play; the job of the economic analyst is to assess the policies without regard to who make them.

This book is a substantially expanded and revised version of a study sponsored by the International Centre for the Study of East Asian Development (ICSEAD), Kitakyushu, Japan and issued in its discussion paper series (Athukorala, 2000b). I am grateful to ICSEAD for generous financial support and for permission to use material here from the original study. Thanks are also due to the Malaysian Institution of Economic Research (MIER) for providing me with institutional support for undertaking research in Malaysia.

In the process of undertaking the study I received invaluable help from many people. My greatest debt is to Michael Meow-Chung Yap who acted as the Malaysian counterpart of the project. It would have been impossible to complete the study without Michael's unfailing support in gathering data from various Malaysian sources and keeping me informed on a regular basis of rapidly unfolding events in Malaysia.

I have profited from ideas and criticisms of many friends at various stages of writing and rewriting the book. Among them Mohamed Ariff, Max Corden, Harold Crouch, Ross Garnaut, Khoo Boo Keit, Hal Hill, Sisira Jayasuriya, Linda Lim, Chris Manning, Suresh Narayanan, Ramakishen Rajan, David Vines and Peter Warr deserve special mention. I am particularly grateful for their willingness to share their insights. My gratitude also goes to Dymphna Evans, the sponsoring editor of Edward Elgar Publishing, for her unfailing enthusiasm in speedy publication of the book.

Finally, I thank my family – Soma, Chintana and Chaturica – for love, unwavering support and endless tolerance.

Chandra Athukorala
Australian National University
June 2001

Abbreviations

BIS	Bank for International Settlements
BLR	Base lending rate
BNM	Bank Negara Malaysia (the Malaysian central bank)
CIC	Corporate Issues Committee
CLOB	Central limit order book market (Singapore)
CPI	Consumer price index
FDI	Foreign direct investment
FOB	Free on board
HPAEs	High Performing Asian Economies
IMF	International Monetary Fund
KLCI	Kuala Lumpur Composite Index
KLSE	Kuala Lumpur Stock Exchange
MGS	Malaysian government securities
MNE	Multinational enterprise
MSCI index	Morgan Stanley Capital International index
NBER	National Bureau of Economic Research (the USA)
NEAC	National Economic Advisory Council
NEP	New Economic Policy
NER	Nominal exchange rate
NERP	National Economic Recovery Plan
NFPEs	Non-finance public enterprises
NPL	Non-performing loan
PPI	Producer (wholesale) price index
RER	Real exchange rate
RM	Malaysian ringgit
SC	Securities Commission
SES	Singapore Stock Exchange
SRR	Statutory reserve requirement
UMNO	United Malay National Organisation
WPI	Wholesale price index

Unless otherwise stated, all monetary units are in nominal terms.

1. State of the debate

The orthodox thinking on capital account convertibility that held sway during the Bretton Woods era was rather cautious of liberalization initiatives in developing countries.[1] The consensus view was that capital account opening should be done cautiously and only after substantial progress has been made in restoring macroeconomic stability, liberalizing the trade account, labour market reforms and establishing a strong regulatory framework to foster a robust domestic financial system. Abrupt dismantling of capital controls at an early stage of reforms without achieving these pre-conditions was thought to be a recipe for exchange rate overvaluation, financial fragility (distorted domestic financial institutions) and eventual economic collapse. This view received ample empirical support from dismal economic outcomes of haphazard liberalization reforms in the late 1970s in many Latin American countries, in particular countries in the Southern cone (Edwards, 1984; Corbo and de Melo, 1987; Michaely *et al.*, 1991; McKinnon, 1991).

There was, however, a clear shift in policy emphasis in favour of greater capital account opening from about the late 1980s, with the IMF and the US Treasury adopting this view as a basic tenet of their policy advocacy for developing countries (Bhagwati, 1998a; Rodrik, 1999).[2] This new policy emphasis was reflected in a major decision by the International Monetary Fund (IMF) to pursue capital account opening as one of its operational objectives. In September 1997, at its annual meeting in Hong Kong, the Interim Committee of the IMF adopted a statement requesting the executive board of the fund to work on an amendment to the IMF Article of Agreement with a view to extending the definition of currency convertibility in the Fund's articles (which is currently limited to current account transactions) to capital account transactions as well.

The push towards capital market opening in developing countries has, however, come under serious reconsideration in the aftermath of the onset of the Asian currency crisis. The fact that several of the Asian nations most affected by the crisis had for some years received substantial flows of foreign capital has raised questions about the role of capital inflows in creating the conditions that generated the crisis or facilitated its dissemination. There has been a huge swing in informed opinion towards thinking that those countries which still maintain closed capital account regimes should undertake the liberalization of short-term capital movements only gradually and with extreme caution (Bhagwati, 1998a; Eichengreen, 1999; Furman and Stiglitz, 1998; Radelet and Sachs, 1998; Williamson, 1999). And even the IMF, despite its continued flirting with mandatory capital account convertibility, has recently become more sympathetic to this cautious approach to capital account opening (IMF, 1999b; Fischer, 1998, 1999).

Despite this new consensus on a more cautious approach to capital account opening, economists are divided on policy options for the East Asian 'crisis countries' (Thailand, Indonesia, Korea, Malaysia and the Philippines) and a few other developing countries, which have already embraced considerable capital account convertibility. The majority opinion seems to be that these countries must contemplate taking precautionary measures against possible disruptive effects of volatile capital flows, instead of making a U-turn to capital controls. A rapidly expanding literature has focused on both precautionary measures that can be taken by individual countries on their own initiative and international initiatives to reform the international financial architecture with a view to taming capital flows at the global level (Eichengreen, 1999; Eichengreen and Mussa, 1998).

Krugman (1998b, 1999b) added variety to the debate by arguing in favour of the Keynesian advocacy of using capital controls as a means of regaining macroeconomic policy autonomy in countries where the currency crisis has rapidly translated into painful economic collapse. By 1998, about a year after the onset of the Asian crisis, there was a growing concern among policy circles that the IMF prescription that placed overwhelming emphasis on confidence building though fiscal and monetary restraint was not working in the crisis-affected countries. Some economists argued that the IMF actually made the crisis worse than it needed to be. These reassessments resulted in a growing consensus in favour of Keynesian reflationary policies. However, any independent policy shift in favour of reflationary policies could have had disastrous consequences because market players are usually suspicious of policies of individual countries which are inconsistent with IMF prescription. The end result would have been intensification of capital flights and exchange rate collapse, leading to a dangerous devaluation–inflation spiral. At the same time, there was a growing conviction in policy circles that economic collapse in the crisis-affected countries had already gone far beyond the actual adjustment warranted by relevant economic fundamentals, because of the self-fulfilling nature of the market panic. In this context, Krugman invoked the conventional textbook wisdom of preventing capital flight through direct government action (capital control) in order to provide policy makers with breathing space to engineer recovery through the Keynesian therapy and to carry out the required fundamental adjustments in an orderly fashion.

Despite endorsement by some notable economists (for example, Barro, 1998; Corden, 1998; Stiglitz, 1999), this advocacy was treated with scepticism by many others. The critics argued that controls on outflows are unlikely to bring about macroeconomic policy autonomy, given difficulties involved in the actual implementation of such controls. They also pointed to various possible growth-retarding effects of such controls. These included their potential to be a source of bad government and corruption on a large scale and potential adverse impact on general investor confidence that may discourage desirable inflows, in particular foreign direct investment (Eichengreen, 1999; DeLong, 1999).

PURPOSE AND SCOPE

The present study intends to inform the policy debate on capital account convertibility in developing countries, relating to both timing and sequencing of economic liberalization reforms and the use of capital controls in crisis management, through a case study of Malaysia. The Malaysian experience provides an excellent laboratory to investigate these issues, given the nature of policy shifts relating to capital account opening immediately before and after the onset of the crisis. The considerable build-up of short-term borrowing and massive foreign investment in share dealing in Malaysia in the mid-1990s, which presumably set the stage for the onset of the crisis, followed hard on the heels of significant liberalization initiatives. In this, the Malaysian experience is remarkably similar to that of the other 'crisis' countries in the region. However, Malaysia is unique among these countries in terms of the strategy that it has chosen to manage the crisis. Unlike the other four countries in East Asia (Thailand, Indonesia, the Philippines and South Korea), which choose to follow the conventional (IMF) reforms, Malaysia responded to the crisis by taking an unorthodox (and risky) policy posture whose key elements were capital controls and expansionary macroeconomic policy.

The methodology is eclectic. There is no single well-specified model that can be used to address the issues at hand. The only meaningful research strategy available to us is to undertake an intensive 'case study' in the context of a broad analytical framework developed by combining the standard open-economy macroeconomic theory and counterfactuals derived from the existing empirical literature on policy response to financial crises in other countries. This approach aims to develop a comprehensive *analytical account* of the onset of the crisis, policy responses and economic adjustment, through a careful examination of cause-and-effect relationships between economic and political variables as they relate to the interactions of capital flows and macroeconomic performance.

To gain perspectives, the Malaysian experience will be compared and contrasted where relevant with the other crisis-hit countries in East Asia, while giving due attention to potentially important inter-country differences relating to the economic structure and the policy context. In discussing economic circumstances leading to the crisis, comparative analysis will make use of data from all the other four crisis-hit countries – Thailand, the Philippines, Indonesia and South Korea (henceforth referred to as Korea) – as well as some countries in the region which experienced only the ripple effect of the crisis. But in discussing the recovery process comparisons will be made only with Korea and Thailand. These two countries, which by and large have followed the conventional (IMF) reform in response to the crisis, provide useful comparators for a study of the outcome of the unorthodox (capital control-based) Malaysian response to the crisis. By contrast, Indonesia is not an appropriate comparator because political instability and social upheaval had interrupted crisis management in that country during most of the period under study. There is also little to gain from a comparison with the Philippines. Economic disruption caused by the mid-1997 speculative attack was relatively small in the Philippines because it had not accumulated volatile foreign capital and had not experienced a real estate boom or a share market bubble to the extent that had occurred in the other four countries. Given the relatively minor disruptions caused by the currency collapse, the Philippines economy had already returned to the pre-crisis growth path by mid-1998.

The data presented in the book come from standard official sources. An attempt has been made to use the same source for each concept and to document carefully the definitions and data sources in the corresponding notes. Unless otherwise stated, the data used in the book come from the Bank Negara Malaysia (BNM) *Monthly Statistical Bulletin* and its regular updates available on the BNM website (*http://www.bnm.gov.my*).

PREVIEW

The book is divided into nine chapters. The second chapter provides an overview of policy trends, growth performance and structural changes in the post-independence Malaysian economy in order to set the stage for the ensuing analysis. Two key themes running though the chapter are the role of Malaysia's long-standing commitment to open trade and foreign direct investment regimes in its impressive growth performance, and the challenges of economic management in a pluralistic society, which dictated strict adherence to a comprehensive affirmative action policy to usher in sociopolitical harmony needed for sustained growth.

Chapter 3 discusses the process of capital account liberalization and other government initiatives to promote Kuala Lumpur as a regional financial centre from the late 1980s. It is noted that these initiatives, undertaken against the backdrop of rapid globalization of world financial markets, set the stage for Malaysia to become a depository for a massive volume of volatile capital, mostly in the form of portfolio investment by the mid-1990s. These capital inflows were instrumental in fuelling the biggest share market boom in any emerging market economy. However, thanks to prudential regulations implemented by Bank Negara Malaysia (the central bank), Malaysia, unlike the other crisis-hit countries, did not accumulate massive short-term bank borrowings.

Chapter 4 attempts to relate capital inflows to other relevant macroeconomic variables to identify the signs of vulnerability of the Malaysian economy to a speculative attack. The analysis identifies massive accumulation of volatile capital relative to national foreign reserves, banking sector fragility and real exchange rate appreciation as the key factors in making the economy vulnerable to the financial crisis. The comparative analysis of the experiences of the other four crisis-hit countries, and Taiwan and Singapore, suggests that in terms of the signs of vulnerability there was remarkable similarity among the five crisis countries. The only notable peculiarity of Malaysia was its remarkably low accumulation of short-term debts, which provided Malaysia with a significant degree of freedom in deciding its own course of crisis management.

Chapter 5 discusses the spread of the Asian crisis to Malaysia, and the initial policy responses, highlighting their political and institutional underpinnings. It also examines the nature and severity of economic collapse and the factors that set the stage for the October 1998 policy turnaround.

Chapter 6 describes the new policy package. It is argued that, given Malaysian policy makers' reluctance to follow an IMF-sponsored reform process which was rooted in the country's policy history, the capital control-based recovery package was a logical policy choice. The policy makers resorted to comprehensive capital controls and fixed the exchange rate in order to gain a breathing space to speed up recovery through fiscal pump priming and expansionary monetary policy, and to restructure the debt-ridden domestic banks and corporations. Capital control measures were carefully aimed at pure financial flows, without encroaching on the long-standing open trade and foreign direct investment regimes.

Chapter 7 looks at the recovery process under the new policy orientation. The Malaysian economy contracted by 7.5 per cent in 1998: the biggest economic collapse ever in the post-independence era. The recession bottomed in the third quarter of 1998. In 1999, the economy recorded a growth rate of 5.4 per cent and regained the pre-crisis level of output by mid-2000. While export-oriented manufacturing played a key role, the recovery was broad-based, with domestic-oriented manufacturing as well as services and construction sectors contributing to GDP growth.

Chapter 8 examines the role of capital controls in the recovery process. The analysis suggests that the carefully designed capital control measures were successful in providing Malaysian policy makers with a viable setting for undertaking Keynesian reflationary policies without adverse backwash effects on foreign direct investment. Controls also assisted banking and corporate restructuring by facilitating the mobilization of domestic resources and, more importantly, by providing a cushion against possible adverse impact on market sentiment of 'national' initiatives in the area of corporate and banking restructuring.

The final chapter draws inferences and policy lessons. Much of the recent debate on the Malaysian 'experiment' has focused largely on the issue of whether the controls have played a 'special role' in delivering a recovery outcome in Malaysia *superior* to that achieved in the IMF programme countries. But when we examine this pragmatic policy choice in the particular sociopolitical setting and the policy history of Malaysia, the real issue is whether the capital control-based reform package was instrumental in achieving recovery while minimizing economic disruptions and related social costs. Viewed from this realistic perspective, by and large the Malaysian experiment has been a success. Of course other countries should be cautious in deriving policy lessons from Malaysia because a number of factors specific to Malaysia seem to have significantly conditioned the outcome of the capital control-based recovery package.

To assist the reader in following the unfolding events, a comprehensive chronology of financial, economic and political events surrounding the crisis is provided in the Appendix (Table A-1).

NOTES

1. The literature on this subject is vast. For authoritative surveys with extensive referencing to the relevant literature see McKinnon (1991), Edwards (1984) and Krueger (1984).
2. Causes of this shift in policy emphasis, which occurred despite the strong mainstream position in support of careful sequencing of reforms (as outlined in the previous paragraph), still remain a moot point. Bhagwati (1998a) argues that the 'Treasury–Wall Street complex' (the confluence of people and thoughts between Wall Street, the US Treasury and the IMF) was the driving force behind it. In line with Bhagwati's view, Stiglitz (who served on the Council of Economic Advisors to the US President during 1993–7) recently noted that 'Treasury pushed liberalization in Korea in 1993 over the opposition of the Council of Economic Advisors' (Stiglitz, 2000). Some identify the weakening of operational relations between the World Bank (which has continued to stick to the orthodox policy advocacy)

and the IMF (whose policy stance has always been predominantly 'balance of payments-centred') as a key factor. To others it is simply a part of the resurgence of free-market ideology following the collapse of the Iron Curtain – the capitalist victory over planned economies.

2. Pre-crisis Malaysian economy: an overview

The purpose of this chapter is to review Malaysia's development experience in historical perspective in order to set the stage for the ensuing analysis. The chapter falls broadly into two parts. The first section traces evolution of economic policy during the post-independence period up to the onset of the recent financial crisis. The next section reviews Malaysia's overall economic performance and structural changes, with emphasis on the rapid growth phase from the late 1980s. A key theme running through the chapter is the dilemma faced by the Malaysian policy makers in achieving rapid growth through increased internationalization of production and trade, while preserving social harmony in a heterogeneous multi-ethnic society.

POLICY CONTEXT

At independence (*Merdeka*) in 1957, economic conditions in Malaysia (then the Federation of Malaya[1]) appeared conducive to rapid and sustained growth. The colonial inheritance included well-developed infrastructure, an efficient administrative mechanism and a thriving primary export sector with immense potential for expansion. In terms of per capita income, literacy and health care, Malaysia was well ahead of most of its neighbours. Although the rate of population increase was already rapid, the highly favourable ratio of land and other natural resources to total population offered great potential to raise income per head.

The mobilization of this development potential for building the new independent Malaysian economy had to be done, however, under conflicting challenges posed by a plural society inherited from its colonial past. At the time the native Malays, who accounted for 52 per cent of the population, dominated politics, but were relatively poor, and were involved mostly in low-productivity agricultural activities.[2] The ethnic Chinese (37 per cent of the population) enjoyed greater economic power and dominated most of the modern-sector activities, but did not match the ethnic solidarity or political power of the Malays. Thus economic policy making in post-independence Malaysia turned out to be *a continuing struggle to achieve development objectives while preserving communal harmony and political stability.*

Government policy during the first decade following independence is perhaps best described as a 'holding' programme, designed to suppress simmering intercommunal rivalries. The policy thrust was to continue with the colonial open-door policy stance relating to trade and industry, while attempting to redress ethnic and regional economic imbalances through rural development schemes and the provision of social and physical infrastructure.

Economic expansion during this period, although respectable, failed to make a substantial contribution towards solving the 'special' problems of the Malays. With urban unemployment rising and education and language again looming as issues, non-Malays began to question the extent to which their interests were being safeguarded in the new Malaysia. The disenchantment growing among all segments of the population ultimately erupted in the bloody communal riots of 13 May 1969. This event produced a clear shift in development strategy away from policy making based purely on economic considerations towards an affirmative action policy based on ethnicity (Leigh, 1992; Jesudason, 1989; Snodgrass, 1995).

The Malay political leaders, who were the dominant group in the ruling coalition (Alliance Party), decided that the ground rules for governance had to be changed. When parliamentary government was restored in February 1971, the constitution was amended to make seditious public discussion of constitutional provisions for language, citizenship, the special position of Malays and the status of the Malay rulers (sultans). Thus the discussion of sensitive constitutional issues was removed from political debate. In the economic sphere, there was a clear shift in the focus of policy making away from pure economic considerations and towards affirmative actions based on ethnicity. This policy shift was formalized in a bold affirmative action policy package under the label of New Economic Policy (NEP) to be implemented over a period of 20 years.

The overriding objective of NEP, launched in 1971, was to maintain national unity through the pursuance of two objectives: eradication of poverty among the entire population and restructuring of society with a view to eliminating the identification of race with economic function. For the first objective, the overall development strategy was reformulated with emphasis on export-oriented industrialization and an ambitious rural development programme. For the second objective, long-term targets were established for the Malay ownership of share capital in limited companies, and the proportion of Malays employed in manufacturing and occupying managerial positions. The NEP aimed to increase the Malay share in corporate assets from 2 per cent in 1970 to 30 per cent in 1990, and to have employment patterns in the urban sector reflect the racial composition of the country. Malay participation in business was to be promoted in two ways: (a) through the expansion of the public sector where Malays held most of the key positions, and (b) by providing Malays with privileged access to share ownership and business opportunities in the private sector. A massive education programme was launched to provide native Malays with scholarships for overseas education and preferential access to placements in local universities.

An Industrial Coordination Act (ICA) was enacted in 1975 to strengthen measures to implement NEP norms on Bumiputra participation at the enterprise level. Under the ICA, the conduct of medium- and large-scale enterprises was subject to licensing with the aim of improving the relative position of the Malays in the modern sector of the economy. Transferring a progressively large share of foreign-owned plantation companies to the nationals was another key element of new policy. However, the government expressed its firm commitment to the practice of transferring ownership through formal share trading rather than through arbitrary expropriation.

There was a heavy emphasis on promotion of heavy industries through direct government involvement in the first half of 1980s, as part of new Prime Minister Mahathir's[3] 'Look East' policy (Crouch, 1996, p. 118). The Heavy Industries Corporation of Malaysia (HICOM), a public sector holding company, was formed in 1980 to go into partnership with foreign companies in setting up industries in areas such as petrochemicals, iron and steel, cement, paper, machinery and equipment, general engineering, transport equipment and building materials. Even though the new selective industrialization push was often rationalized as an attempt to emulate Japan and Korea, in practice the selection of new projects was based largely on traditional import-substitution criteria. These projects were supported by subsidized credit, government procurement provisions and heavy tariff protection.[4] Despite this emphasis on promoting heavy industries via public sector participation, Malaysian policy makers stayed clear of quantitative import restrictions as a policy tool.

The rapid expansion of public expenditure as a result of massive government investment programmes under the new industrialization drive and the implementation of various NEP programmes was reflected in widening budget and current account deficits between 1981 and 1986. The macro imbalance was compounded by deterioration in the terms of trade owing to adverse trends in prices of Malaysia's major export products in the context of world recession in the mid-1980s (Corden, 1996; Narayanan, 1996). These factors brought the economic advances of the 1970s to a halt. After almost one-and-a-half decades of policy emphasis, there seemed but a slim chance of the NEP's targets being achieved on schedule in 1990. With a rapid increase in unemployment, race relations became increasingly tense and many even feared a possible replay of the events of 13 May 1969 (Crouch, 1998).[5] Political and policy uncertainty was reflected in stagnation in private investment (both local and foreign) in the economy.

This volatile climate paved the way for a series of policy reforms, which placed greater emphasis on the role of the private sector and strengthening the conditions for export-oriented industrialization through greater participation of foreign direct investment (FDI). The new policy orientation involved the easing of some strictures of the NEP, with a view to making wealth creation more important than wealth redistribution. The Promotion of Investment Act of 1986 introduced fresh, more generous incentives for private investors, and some of the ethnic requirements of the NEP were relaxed. In particular, the commitment to the 30 per cent equity participation target became more flexible. Up to 100 per cent foreign equity ownership of export-oriented companies was allowed.

At the end of its 20-year implementation period, the NEP was extended with some modifications for a further decade in 1990 under the new label of National Development Policy (NDP). The NDP reflected a switch in the government's approach towards support for the Malay community. It placed greater emphasis on redressing racial imbalance in a more overt fashion through various initiatives geared to entrepreneurship, managerial expertise and skills development within the Malay community (Ariff, 1991). This difference notwithstanding, NDP reaffirmed the continuation of the strong affirmative action policy of the NEP as the basic tenet of overall government policy.

The reforms from the mid-1980s also involved a gradual process of privatization and restructuring of state-owned enterprises. By the early 1990s, state ownership in manufacturing was limited only to some politically sensitive ventures in car manufacturing, petrochemicals, iron and steel and cement industries.

In the area of labour market reforms, there was a new emphasis (like that of the East Asian newly industrialized countries) on job creation rather than the protection of workers' rights through labour legislation. To this end, attempts were made to achieve labour market flexibility through industrial relations legislation, which provided for compulsory arbitration of disputes and prohibition of strikes in 'essential services'. Furthermore, unions were banned in the most important export-oriented industry – electronics – until 1988, after which only 'in-house' unions were allowed at the plant, rather than the industry, level. This labour market policy, despite its many critics, has certainly facilitated the outward-oriented growth process with foreign capital participation.[6]

A firm commitment to an open trade regime continued to be an integral part of the overall development strategy.[7] Tariff protection of domestic manufacturing, which had always been low relative to many other developing countries, was further reduced over time. The average effective rate of manufacturing protection, which increased from about 25 per cent in the early 1960s to 70 per cent in the early 1970s, declined continuously thereafter, coming down to below 30 per cent by the late 1980s (Alavi, 1996, Tables 3.2, 3.3 and 7.2). By the mid-1990s, only 3 per cent of all import tariff lines were subject to licensing requirements and the import-value weighted average nominal tariff was as low as 15 per cent.

The market-oriented policy reforms were accompanied by a strong focus on restoring and maintaining macroeconomic stability (Corden, 1996; Salleh and Meyanathan, 1993). The Fifth (1986–90) and Sixth (1991–5) Malaysia Plans saw a significant reduction in overall government expenditure and a shift in government spending away from public sector enterprises and towards infrastructure projects designed to enhance private sector development. Throughout the ensuing decade, budgetary restraints on operating expenditure were an important aspect of fiscal policy. Budget deficit was always kept within prudent limits while minimizing the use of borrowed funds. When overall deficits arose occasionally as a result of higher development expenditure, they were financed from non-inflationary domestic sources, in particular private savings accumulated in the Employees' Provident Fund. Broadening of the tax base and the good performance of the economy, coupled with greater efficiency in tax collection, contributed to the increase in government revenue. Increased revenue and prudent expenditure management made it possible for the federal government to reduce external borrowing and even to repay the more expensive external loans well before the due dates.

Bank Negara Malaysia (the central bank) embarked on a tight monetary policy stance from about 1988 to accommodate fiscal prudence. The conduct of monetary policy, while maintaining a quasi-pegged exchange rate regime, became more complicated owing to debilitating elements endogenous to the rapid growth process. Rising demand for credit in a booming economy tended to widen interest rate differentials in Malaysia's favour. This, coupled with rapid globalization of capital markets, triggered large capital inflows – mostly short-term funds – putting pressure on the exchange rate. Despite these challenges, the central bank managed to mop up excess liquidity in the domestic economy through a combination of direct money market intervention and continued centralization of excess government funds.

In sum, despite challenges involved in meeting conflicting objectives in a plural society, Malaysian policy makers have by and large been successful in positioning Malaysia within the new world economic order characterized by increased internationalization of production. While there were some policy excesses triggered by ethnic considerations, they never resorted to stringent restrictions on foreign trade or foreign direct investment. Despite affirmative action policies under the NEP, the private sector was never marginalized and the policy emphasis on export orientation was never compromised. This policy regime, coupled with a stable political climate, enabled the Malaysian economy to take full advantage of the new opportunities arising from integration with the global economy.

ECONOMIC PERFORMANCE

Growth and Structural Change

At the time of independence in 1957, Malaysia had the highest per capita income in the Asia–Pacific region, excepting Japan (Table 2.1). During the

Table 2.1 Economic growth: Malaysia and other Asian economies

	GNP per capita relative to the USA (%)				GNP growth (%)		Per capita GDP growth (%)	
	1955	1960	1987	1996	1960–95	1987–96	1965–96	1987–96
East Asia	—	17.1	59.2	72.3	8.3	6.3	6.9	5.8
Hong Kong	—	21.0	73.0	98.5	7.0	5.4	6.1	4.8
South Korea	8.9	8.7	29.8	48.9	8.6	8.0	6.9	7.2
Singapore	—	16.6	53.3	85.4	8.4	8.2	6.8	6.3
Taiwan	—	13.8	46.7	56.2	7.9	7.5	6.5	6.4
China	—	3.1	5.2	10.8	6.8	9.4	8.6	11.3
Southeast Asia	—	9.7	15.9	21.3	6.2	7.3	3.9	5.7
Indonesia	—	5.8	9.6	13.2	6.6	7.0	4.5	5.5
Malaysia	14.2	15.0	21.7	37.2	7.1	10.2	4.6	7.8
Philippines	10.7	11.5	9.3	9.5	3.7	2.9	1.2	0.3
Thailand	7.4	9.6	15.6	25.6	6.8	8.4	4.4	7.1
South Asia	—	8.1	7.8	9.5	4.2	5.2	1.9	3.1
Bangladesh	—	9.2	7.2	8.7	3.6	5.3	1.2	3.3
India	6.5	7.4	6.5	8.2	4.2	5.2	1.9	3.2
Pakistan	6.2	6.8	7.5	7.8	5.2	4.0	2.2	1.3
Sri Lanka	12.5	12.5	11.7	13.1	4.3	7.3	2.6	5.9

Note: — Data not available.

Source: Author's computations based on *Penn World Tables*, mark 5.6 (accessed via worldwide web page of the National Bureau of Economic Research). Data for 1993–6 are extrapolations of 1992 values based on growth rates from *International Financial Statistics Yearbook 1998*, Washington, DC: IMF.

next two decades Malaysia's ranking dropped as a result of dramatic economic expansion in the four East Asian newly industrialized countries (NICs). The annual growth rate of real gross domestic product (GDP) during the period 1965–86 averaged 5.5 per cent, an impressive figure by developing country standards, yet performance was uneven over time, reflecting the impact of primary commodity cycles and changes in government expenditure. For instance, the growth rate averaged about 6.5 per cent per annum during the 1970s, but then slowed in the first half of the 1980s and fell to minus 1 per cent in 1985.

Following the far-reaching structural adjustment reforms undertaken in response to the events of the mid-1980s, the Malaysian economy entered a decade of unprecedented growth in 1988. During this period Malaysia recorded the second-highest gross national product (GNP) growth rate (both in per capita and in absolute terms) in the Asian region after China (which in any case started rapid growth from a relatively low base). Purchasing power parity (PPP)-adjusted per capita income relative to the USA increased from 22 per cent to 37 per cent between 1987 and 1996. Malaysia's performance during this period looks particularly impressive in comparison with the Philippines and Sri Lanka, which had comparable initial income levels coupled with a significant lead over Malaysia in terms of human capital endowments and, perhaps, superior administrative mechanisms. Outside the region the only country which has matched (or surpassed in some years) Malaysia's growth record during this period is diamond-rich Botswana (Snodgrass, 1995).

As in the other high performing East Asian countries (HPAEs),[8] rapid export orientation was central to Malaysia's economic transformation. The 'export coefficient' (total merchandise exports as a percentage of GDP)[9] increased from about 50 per cent in the mid-1980s to over 95 per cent by the mid-1990s (Table 2.2). In the 1990s, Malaysia's export coefficient was the third highest in the developing world after Singapore (over 170 per cent) and Hong Kong (over 140 per cent) (Krugman, 1995).

In the 1970s and early 1980s, Malaysian economic growth was predominantly accounted for by the expansion of service industries emanating from public sector activities and growth in primary production (Table 2.3). Since the late 1980s, not only has there been a significant increase in growth, but much of it is has come from the expansion of manufacturing through private sector initiatives. In 1989, for the first time, the manufacturing share in GDP overtook that of agriculture. Between 1987 and 1996, the manufacturing sector grew by an average annual rate of 14 per cent, with the share of manufacturing in GDP increasing from about 20 per cent to over 34 per cent. Between these two years, over 50 per cent of the growth in GDP came directly from the manufacturing sector. In addition, much of the output and expansion in the tertiary (service) sector in recent years has been closely

Table 2.2 Malaysia: selected economic indicators, 1980 and 1985–97

	1980	1985	1986	1987	1988	1989	1990	1991	1992	1993	1994	1995	1996	1997
Real GDP growth	7.44	–0.96	1.05	5.39	8.94	9.21	9.74	8.66	7.79	8.34	8.75	9.62	8.23	8.04
Per capita income ($)	1 723	1 850	1 607	1 793	1 933	2 053	2 307	2 491	2 925	3 174	3 505	4 133	4 449	4 315
Real per capita income growth	4.07	–3.55	–1.65	2.71	6.3	6.63	7.21	6.15	5.3	4.74	4.41	6.7	5.7	5.5
Unemployment rate	5.6	6.9	8.3	8.2	8.1	6.3	5.1	4.3	3.7	3.0	2.9	2.8	2.5	2.5
Inflation rate (CPI-based)	6.7	0.3	0.8	0.2	2.5	2.7	2.8	2.6	4.7	3.5	3.7	3.4	3.5	2.7
Money supply (M2) growth (%)	28.4	9.8	11.0	3.8	6.7	15.2	10.6	16.9	29.2	26.6	12.7	20.0	23.8	18.9
Average commercial bank deposit rate (%)	6.0	7.5	7.0	4.3	4.3	5.4	7.2	8.2	7.8	6.3	6.2	6.9	7.3	8.2
Gross domestic investment (% of GDP)	30.4	27.6	26.0	23.2	25.9	28.4	31.3	37.2	33.5	37.8	40.4	43.5	41.5	42.8
Gross domestic saving (% of GDP)	29.3	25.6	25.6	31.3	31.3	29.2	29.2	28.4	29.7	33.0	32.6	33.8	37.1	37.2
Fiscal balance (% of GDP)	–6.9	–5.7	–10.5	–7.7	–3.6	–3.3	–3.0	–2.0	–0.8	0.2	2.3	0.9	0.7	2.4
Public debt (% of GDP)	44.0	82.4	103.4	103.5	98.0	87.8	81.4	74.6	65.6	58.0	48.9	41.8	35.9	32.5
Foreign debt (% of total)	20.7	36.1	38.3	33.5	29.1	26.9	25.7	25.5	21.6	20.2	15.9	14.6	11.7	14.4
Export/GDP ratio (%)	51.47	54.85	56.31	63.85	67.61	73.26	76.28	80.84	77.65	81.45	89.82	95.5	92.01	89.76
Growth of export value ($) (%)	17.1	–7.7	–10.5	30.9	17.4	18.1	16.6	17.1	18.1	16.1	23.1	26.5	7.4	0.7
Growth of import value ($) (%)	33.6	14.1	10.6	15.8	28.6	31.7	28.4	26.9	10.1	17.8	28.1	30.3	1.9	1.2
Current account balance (% of GDP)	–1.1	–1.9	–0.4	8.1	5.4	0.8	–2.1	–8.8	–3.8	–4.8	–7.8	–9.7	–4.4	–5.6
Total external debt (% of GDP)	28.8	54.8	70.5	63.2	51.7	44.3	39.7	38.5	37.9	41.9	38.7	38.9	39.2	61.6
Short-term debt (% of total)	—	—	—	—	5.2	7.4	9.6	14.1	23.5	25.0	19.3	19.1	25.7	25.3
Debt service ratio, total (%)	4.3	15.8	18.9	16.4	13.1	9.6	8.3	6.9	9.3	6.4	5.5	6.6	6.9	5.5
Debt service ratio, federal government (%)	1.8	6.7	7.2	5.9	6.2	4.4	1.2	2.7	4.2	2.8	1.4	1.4	1.1	0.7
Foreign reserves, end of year ($bn)	4.4	4.9	6.0	7.4	6.5	7.8	9.8	10.9	17.2	27.2	25.4	23.8	27.0	20.8

Note: — data not available.

Source: Compiled from IMF, *International Financial Statistics Yearbook 1988* and BNM, *Monthly Statistical Bulletin*, March 1999.

*Table 2.3 Sectoral growth performance: contribution to GDP and real growth rates (in brackets), 1970–96**

	1970	1975	1980	1985	1990	1996
Agriculture	28.5	26.9	22.9	20.8	18.7	12.6
	—	(9.5)	(5.1)	(3.1)	(4.6)	(2.5)
Industry	32.3	32.6	35.8	36.7	42.2	41.3
	—	(6.7)	(10.7)	(5.7)	(9.8)	(12.7)
Manufacturing	15.8	17.3	19.6	19.5	26.9	34.2
	—	(6.7)	(11.4)	(5.3)	(13.7)	(13.2)
Services**	33.5	40.5	41.3	42.6	39.1	38.9
	—	(12.2)	(13.9)	(5.8)	(5.1)	(9.2)
Total	100	100	100	100	100	100
	—	(10.6)	(8.5)	(5.2)	(6.8)	(8.4)

Notes:
* output shares and growth rates are based on constant (1978) prices. Growth rates are annual averages between the reported years.
** Include import duties net of bank service charges.
— Data not available.

Source: Ministry of Finance Malaysia, *Economic Report* (various issues).

related to the expansion of the manufacturing sector (Ariff, 1991). The share of agriculture declined from 30 per cent to 12 per cent.[10]

The expansion of manufacturing came predominantly from production for exporting. The ratio of exports to total production (gross output) in manufacturing increased from around 10 per cent in the early 1970s to over 65 per cent by the mid-1990s (Athukorala and Menon, 1999). Rapid export orientation of domestic manufacturing brought about a dramatic transformation in Malaysia's export structure, which historically had been dominated by a limited range of primary commodities. In the early 1970s, the share of manufactures in total merchandise exports was about 10 per cent. Since then, manufactured exports have emerged as the most dynamic element in the export structure. Exports of manufactures grew (in current US dollar terms) at an annual compound rate of 35 per cent during the period 1980–96. By the mid-1990s, with a manufacturing share of about 78 per cent in total exports, Malaysia was the developing world's sixth-largest exporter of manufactures, after the four East Asian newly industrialized countries and China.

Foreign direct investment (FDI) played a pivotal role in the expansion of manufacturing production and in particular manufacturing exports. Foreign firms accounted for over 45 per cent of total manufacturing value added and they accounted for over three-quarters of total manufactured exports by the mid-1990s (Athukorala, 1998a, ch. 8).

Malaysia's remarkable growth acceleration through export-led industrialization from the late 1980s occurred under conditions of low inflation, both by regional and overall developing country standards (Corden, 1996). Despite continuing demand pressure in a booming economy, the average inflation rate during 1988–96 (3.5 per cent) was only marginally higher than that for the period 1961–88 (3.3%). During the period 1990–96, Malaysia had the second-lowest average annual inflation rate (3.8 per cent) after Singapore (2.3 per cent) among the high performing Asian economies.

Saving, Investment and Fiscal Position

Growth acceleration was underpinned by a rapid increase in domestic capital formation. Gross domestic investment as a ratio of GDP increased from about 28 per cent in the second half of the 1980s to over 40 per cent by the mid-1990s.[11] Rapid capital accumulation did not, however, exert excess pressure on the balance of payments of the country because of the impressive domestic saving performance. Malaysia's national saving rate increased from about 27 per cent to 37 per cent between these two time points, leaving a *resource gap*[12] of only 6 per cent to be financed by running a current account deficit. Moreover, the bulk of this resource gap was covered by net FDI inflows. Thus, in most years a high investment rate could be maintained without accumulating foreign debt. The external debt service ratio (debt repayments and interest payments as a percentage of total export earnings) in fact declined from over 12 per cent in the mid-1980s to less than 7 per cent by the mid-1990s.

For the first time in Malaysian history, the federal government achieved a balanced budget in 1993 and this was maintained in subsequent years. Compared to the 1986–9 period, the public sector was a net saver during the period 1990–96. The fiscal balance as a percentage of GDP turned around from a deficit of 2.5 per cent to a surplus of 1.5 per cent between these two periods. This improvement was attributable largely to higher tax revenue collection concomitant with strong growth, as well as a broader tax base and improvement in efficiency in the tax collection system. Non-finance public enterprises (NFPEs) as a group continued to record a current surplus from the early 1990s. Thus the consolidated public sector current surplus increased from 5.2 per cent to 7.7 per cent of GDP between 1990 and 1996. The overall public sector surplus in 1996 was 7.1 per cent, up from 4.1 per cent in 1990. Unlike the situation in many other developing countries, the budget deficits were not a source of inflation as they were not financed through borrowing from the central bank. As a share of GDP, domestic public debts and external public debt declined dramatically, from 64 per cent to 39 per cent and 23 per cent to 6.6 per cent, respectively, between 1990 and 1996.

Balance of Payments

The current account in Malaysia's balance of payments has traditionally been characterized by surpluses in the merchandise account but persistent deficits in the services account (Table 2.2). In most years until the late 1980s, the trade surplus outweighed the services deficit to yield a current account surplus. This pattern has changed during the rapid growth phase since 1989. Strong growth of the economy led to a surge in imports of capital goods and intermediate inputs. Consequently, the merchandise account surplus was reduced. At the same time, the services account remained in deficits, reflecting a large, net outflow of profit and dividends. Thus the current account balance shifted from surpluses in the late 1980s to growing deficits in the 1990s. To a large extent, the widening of the deficit was a consequence of the strength of investment growth; it is an accounting impossibility for a nation simultaneously to attract large inflows of capital to boost domestic investment and to run a current account surplus. The strength of a nation's external balance must therefore be viewed by the way in which the deficit has been financed. In Malaysia, in most years the strong inflow of long-term FDI was more than sufficient to finance the current account deficit. The basic balance (current account balance plus long-term capital flows) was always in surplus during the period 1990–96, adding to national foreign exchange reserves.

Consequently, there was less need for the nation to resort to large-scale external borrowing (Table 2.4). During the period 1990–98, Malaysia's external (foreign) debt remained between 39 and 42 per cent of GDP, while the debt–service ratio (the ratio of debt payments and interest payments to export earnings) remained below 10 per cent in all years, remarkably low by developing country standards. Reflecting narrowing budget deficits and expanding domestic revenue base, the share of consolidated public debt (federal government plus NFPEs) in total foreign debt declined consistently from over 80 per cent in 1990 to less than 40 per cent in 1996.

Growth, Equity and Social Harmony

In the early 1960s the unemployment rate in peninsular Malaysia was estimated at 6 per cent. By the early 1970s, this had increased to 8 per cent, but the policy makers at the time could offer no more than containment at that level (Snodgrass, 1980, p. 59). After a drop to around 5 per cent in the early 1980s, the unemployment rate continued to increase, reaching a peak of 8.3 per cent in 1986.[13] Thereafter it began to decline, with virtual

Table 2.4 Malaysia: external debt, 1990–98

	1990	1991	1992	1993	1994	1995	1996	1997	1998	1990–96
Total (US$ billion)	17.0	18.5	21.9	26.9	28.1	34.0	39.0	60.8	40.8	26.3[1]
% of GDP	39.6	39.3	37.7	41.9	38.7	38.9	39.2	62.2	91.8	39.3
Composition (%)	100	100	100	100	100	100	100	100	100	100
Medium and long-term debt[2]	90.4	85.9	76.5	75.0	80.7	80.9	74.3	74.7	82.2	79.6
Federal government	53.9	49.9	37.4	28.0	20.1	15.7	10.7	7.6	9.3	27.0
NFPEs[3]	25.7	22.9	20.4	24.6	27.7	32.2	29.9	30.7	33.3	26.9
Private sector	10.8	13.2	18.7	22.4	32.9	33.0	33.7	36.4	39.5	25.7
Short-term debt[4]	9.6	14.1	23.5	25.0	19.3	19.1	25.7	25.3	17.8	20.4
Banking sector	9.6	14.1	23.5	25.0	13.4	13.3	17.4	18.9	12.3	16.8
Non-bank private sector	0.0	0.0	0.0	0.0	6.0	5.8	8.3	6.4	5.5	3.6
External debt–service ratio:[5] Total	8.3	6.9	9.3	6.4	5.5	6.6	6.9	5.5	6.7	7.1
Federal government	—	2.7	4.2	2.8	1.4	1.4	1.1	0.7	1.0	2.3

Notes:
1. Annual average.
2. Debt with a tenure of more than one year.
3. Includes both government guaranteed and non-guaranteed debt of non-financial public enterprises (NFPEs).
4. Debt with a tenure of one year and below.
5. Repayment and interest payment of external debt as a percentage of gross exports of goods and services.
— data not available.

Source: Compiled from Bank Negara Malaysia, *Monthly Statistical Bulletin*, March 1999, Kuala Lumpur.

full-employment being reached by 1996, with unemployment at only 2.8 per cent, the lowest level in 30 years. It is interesting to note that this impressive employment record was achieved in a context of increasing labour force participation of the population. The rate of labour force participation increased from an average level of 65 per cent in 1980–85 to over 67 per cent by the mid-1990s. Most of the new employment opportunities came from the rapidly expanding manufacturing sector. The share of manufacturing in total labour deployment increased from 14 per cent in the mid-1970s to 27 per cent in 1996. The direct contribution of manufacturing to the total increment in employment between 1987 and 1996 was as high as 63 per cent (Athukorala and Menon, 1999).

There was a decline in real wages (measured by average manufacturing earning) in the early 1970s partly reflecting the shift in the structure of production away from capital-intensive import substitution activities and towards labour-intensive export production. At the same time, real wages were kept low by the availability of a vast pool of surplus labour in the economy, particularly in the rural sector. With the gradual absorption of surplus labour in export-oriented industries, real wages started to rise from the late 1970s. The real wage index increased from an average level of 74 in 1975–99 to 105 in 1985. Following a mild decline during the years of macroeconomic adjustment in the mid-1980s, the index increased continuously, reaching a historical high of 121 in 1995. It seems that, in the absence of minimum wage legislation, employment levels rose first, followed by market- and productivity-driven increases in real wages. Interestingly, increase in real wages occurred in a context where the profitability of manufacturing production (as measured by the price–cost margin) remained virtually unchanged. Thus it appears that, with the rapid depletion of surplus labour reserves in the economy, workers have become the major beneficiaries of productivity growth in manufacturing.

Growth in real wages in the 1990s would have presumably been much sharper had it not been for the influx of migrant workers (Athukorala and Manning, 1999). With the approach of full employment, forcing rapid increases in real wages, Malaysia has begun to experience a massive influx of migrant workers from neighbouring labour surplus countries, Indonesia in particular. Official estimates put the number of migrant workers in Malaysia at 650 000 in 1995, but the finance minister stated in his 1997 Budget speech that the total number (both legal and illegal workers) could be as high as 2 million (25 per cent of a (local) labour force of 8 million). By the early 1990s, foreign workers represented over 60 per cent of the workforce on plantations and 70 per cent in the construction industry, and had begun to enter the manufacturing sector in large numbers.

Rapid employment expansion in export-oriented manufacturing and related activities, and the subsequent increase in real wages were instrumental in reducing poverty and promoting equity and social harmony. The incidence of poverty among all households (as measured by the percentage of total households below the poverty line) fell from 18.4 per cent in 1984 to 9.6 per cent in 1995; (Athukorala and Menon, 1995b). A significant decline was observable for both urban and rural households, even though the incidence of poverty is still relatively high in rural areas. All ethnic groups shared in the remarkable improvement in quality of life. While less impressive than with its record in reducing absolute poverty, Malaysia was also successful (by the standards of developing countries at the same stage of development) in addressing inequality in the size distribution of income (relative poverty). Between 1970 and 1995, the Gini coefficient fell from 0.537 to 0.446, suggesting that the benefits of rapid growth spread reasonably widely among various income groups.

CONCLUDING REMARKS

For almost a decade up to the onset of the currency crisis in mid-1997, the Malaysian economy was expanding at an average annual rate of 8 per cent, with low inflation, rapid employment growth and a sound external payments position. Sustained high growth was accompanied by rising living standards with a relatively equal distribution of income, ameliorating the twin problems of poverty and racial imbalances. With this impressive performance record, coupled with political stability and policy continuity, the international community had begun to admire Malaysia as the best 'development success story' among the second-tier newly industrializing economies in East Asia. Many Malaysia observers considered Malaysia's aim of entering the league of developed nations by 2020[14] a realistic target. For over five years, the country's foreign currency sovereign credit rating was an A+, in the same league as Hong Kong.[15]

These expectations were shattered by the onset of the financial crisis in mid-1997, which halted Malaysia's ascendancy for almost three years. Growth of real output (GDP) slowed to 7.5 per cent in 1997 and contracted by 7.5 per cent in the following years. The economy regained the pre-crisis output level only in the second quarter of 2000. The crisis thus added almost three years to the time Malaysia would need to achieve developed-country standards of living.

What happened to Malaysia? Did it simply succumb to a wild speculative attack in the wake of the Thai crisis, or were there some fundamental weaknesses in the pre-crisis Malaysian economy that made it vulnerable to the Thai contagion? The 'official' view, which is also supported by many independent observers, is that the crisis was a mere reflection of the Thai contagion.

However, as we will argue in the next two chapters, when one looks beyond the general performance indicators of the real economy, there is convincing evidence that the contagion was only the 'trigger' factor, and the Malaysian economy succumbed to the crisis because over time it had developed vulnerability to a speculative currency attack. To anticipate the analysis in the next two chapters, massive accumulation of short-term capital (mostly in the form of foreign portfolio investment) at a much faster rate than growth of foreign exchange reserves, coupled with rapid deterioration of financial sector health (financial fragility) and real exchange rate appreciation, were the main sources of Malaysia's vulnerability. These developments were largely a reflection of slippage in macroeconomic management resulting from the 'high growth push' of the government over the past few years. These shortcomings of the policy regime in the lead-up to the crisis remained hidden beneath the impressive performance record, when the period from 1987 was taken as a whole.

NOTES

1. The Federation of Malaya, comprising 11 states in the Malay Peninsula, secured independence from Britain on 31 August 1957. Sabah, Sarawak and Singapore joined Malaya to form Malaysia on 16 September 1963. Singapore left the federation in August 1965.
2. In 1957–8, 34.9 per cent of households had incomes of less than Malaysian ringgit (RM) 120 per month (the official cut-off point for measuring poverty). More than half of these households were Malay, and more than two-thirds were rural (Snodgrass, 1980).
3. Dr Mahathir became prime minister in 1981.
4. By 1987, there were 867 corporate public enterprises in Malaysia, more than a third of which were in manufacturing. The symbol of the selective industrial policy was the Proton (Malaysian car) project which was set up by HICOM in collaboration with the Mitsubishi Corporation in Japan.
5. For an interesting journalistic account of these developments see Rashid (1997, ch. 14).
6. For a lucid discussion of Malaysia's political changes as they relate to the industrialization process, see Chapter 12 in Crouch (1996).
7. In a recent comprehensive study of the patterns and chronology of trade policy reforms during the postwar era, Sachs and Warner (1995, Table 1) identify Malaysia as one of the eight developing countries whose trade regimes remained *open* throughout the period. The other seven countries are Barbados, Cyprus, Hong Kong, Mauritius, Singapore, Thailand and the Yemen Arab Republic.
8. The term 'HPAEs', first used in World Bank (1993), refers to the four 'tiger economies', Hong Kong, South Korea, Singapore and Taiwan, and the three newly industrializing economies in Southeast Asia: Indonesia, Malaysia and Thailand.
9. Note that in calculating this ratio exports have been measured in gross terms while GDP is naturally in value added terms. Given the fact that around 40 per cent of total value added is generated in non-traded sectors, a high trade share of this magnitude simply reflects Malaysia's heavy dependence on production processes which involve adding a fairly small amount of value to intermediate goods, benefiting from the ability of modern industry to slice up the value chain and relocate labour-intensive activities in developing countries (Krugman, 1995).
10. The relative importance of agriculture (in particular the plantations sector) would have

declined even more rapidly had it not been for the influx of foreign workers to meet labour shortages created by the lucrative employment opportunities in the rapidly growing manufacturing sector (Pillai, 1995).

11. According to a careful growth accounting exercise by Gan and Soon (1998), contribution to GDP growth of capital accumulated increased from 38.5 per cent to 52.3 per cent between 1984–9 and 1990–95, against a decline in the contribution of labour from 32.7 per cent to 23.8 per cent, leading to a decline in the contribution of total factor productivity growth from 30.8 per cent to 23.9 per cent. These figures are consistent with the recent controversial interpretation of the East Asian growth as primarily an outcome of capital accumulation rather than improvement in productivity ('perspiration rather than inspiration') (Krugman, 1994). Here we do not intend to pursue this debate because it is only relevant for analysing long-term growth trajectory of these countries, not an economic collapse.
12. The difference between domestic saving and investment which is needed to be financed by running a current account deficit.
13. The unemployment rates reported in this paragraph are surprisingly high by developing country standards, given the relatively rapid rate of growth of the Malaysian economy compared with that of many other developing countries. Mazumdar (1981) ascribes this apparent peculiarity to two special features of the Malaysian economy (which was predominantly a reflection of an extreme case of youth unemployment): prevalence of joint households (a household that supports dependent – non-earning – relatives), which generally encouraged youth unemployment and the relatively small size of the informal sector. This factor may also partly account for the long pre-employment waiting period and high level of open unemployment among school leavers.
14. This was the growth target set by Prime Minister Mahathir in his famous 'Vision 2020' speech, made in 1990.
15. Standard & Poor's foreign currency sovereign credit ratings for the other crisis countries as at the end of May 1997 were: South Korea AA–, Thailand A, Indonesia BBB and Philippine BB+ (*Far Eastern Economic Review*, 29 May, p. 60).

3. Capital account opening, capital inflow and share market boom

As we saw in the previous chapter, Malaysia is unique among developing countries in its long-standing commitment to an open foreign trade regime. As an essential element of the openness to trade, throughout the post-independence period the Malaysian dollar (renamed ringgit in 1975) remained fully convertible for current account transactions. Although exporters were required to convert foreign currency sales proceeds into local currency within six months, this was not a binding constraint on production for export because the import trade regime remained highly liberal. Despite mandatory approval procedures, the exchange rules relating to all current account transactions remained liberal. With this policy orientation, Malaysia achieved Article VIII status (for current account convertibility) under the IMF Articles of Agreement on 11 November 1968, becoming the fourth Asian country to enter this country league after Hong Kong (15 February 1961), Japan (1 April 1964) and Singapore (9 November 1968).[1]

CAPITAL ACCOUNT REGIME

A natural companion to outward-oriented trade policy was a firm commitment to the promotion of foreign direct investment (FDI). FDI approval procedures and restrictions on foreign equity ownership were very liberal by the developing country standards even in the 1950s and 1960s, at a time when hostility towards multinationals was the order of the day in the developing world. As discussed in Chapter 2, emphasis on FDI promotion received added impetus with a notable shift in development policy towards export-oriented industrialization in the early 1970s. The Malaysian policy regime relating to non-FDI capital flows (that is, international flows of purely financial capital) in general, too, was much more liberal throughout the postwar period, compared to most other developing countries (Williamson and Mahar, 1998). However, liberalization in this sphere was much more cautious and gradual by Malaysia's own historical record of trade liberalization.

Most restrictions on short-term overseas investment by residents were removed in the 1970s. By the turn of the decade residents were free to place deposits abroad, lend to non-residents, purchase immobile properties or invest in foreign equity, provided such investments were not financed from borrowing in Malaysia. But there was one important exception: Bank Negara Malaysia (BNM), the central bank, continued to monitor foreign currency borrowings by residents and domestic borrowing by non-residents under borrowing/lending ceilings stipulated in foreign exchange regulations (Yusof *et al.*, 1994; BNM, 1994; Williamson, 1999). At the onset of the financial crisis in mid-1997, the ceilings on foreign currency borrowing by residents and domestic borrowing by non-resident controlled companies stood at 1 million and 10 million Malaysian ringgit (RM) respectively.

Acceleration of Capital Account Opening in the 1990s

Promotion of Kuala Lumpur as a global financial centre became a key element of Malaysia's growth euphoria in the late 1980s. As the first step to give momentum to the growth of Kuala Lumpur Stock Exchange (KLSE)[2] as an independent entity, the government announced on 27 October 1989 delisting (with effect from 2 January 1990) of Malaysian registered companies from the Stock Exchange of Singapore (SES). This split from SES intended to set the stage for developing the KLSE as an independent stock exchange, to attract international investors in competition with SES.[3] The early 1990s saw a number of initiatives to further liberalization of impediments to portfolio capital inflow, to promote the trading on the Kuala Lumpur Stock Exchange with increased participation of institutional investors.

In 1992, the Securities Act was passed to enable the establishment of a new Securities Commission (SC) to take over the share market monitoring and supervision, previously undertaken by the Capital Investment Committee under the jurisdiction of Bank Negara Malaysia. This initiative gave further impetus to stock market growth under a more flexible operational framework. In the same year, the ceiling on foreign share holding of local brokerage firms was lifted from 30 per cent to 49 per cent. Tax rates for both foreign and local fund managers were reduced from 30 per cent to 10 per cent.

The Federal Territory of Labuan was inaugurated as an international offshore financial centre on 1 October 1990.[4] It was envisaged that, with the Asia–Pacific region emerging as the fastest growing region in the world, Labuan would play a key role in enhancing the attractiveness of Malaysia as a world investment centre (BNM, 1994, pp. 45–7). Licensed offshore banks, offshore insurance entities and other offshore companies operating in Labuan were declared as non-residents for exchange control purposes. This initiative enabled these institutions to operate foreign currency accounts freely and move funds into and out of Malaysia without being subject to any exchange control monitoring. Licensed offshore banks were also permitted to accept deposits and grant loans in foreign currency. Investment guidelines were liberalized to allow Malaysian fund management companies to form joint ventures with foreign fund management companies. Management companies of unit trust funds located in Labuan were permitted to invest in Malaysian securities. Generous tax exemption was granted to companies incorporated in Labuan and to their expatriate employees.[5]

The process of capital account opening was temporarily halted in 1994 when the ringgit came under strong buying pressure as the booming economy created expectations about the currency's increasing strength. From late 1993, speculators bought ringgit in large amounts, increasing short-term deposits and forward transactions. In order to avoid an adverse effect on export competitiveness from a sharp exchange rate appreciation, BNM imposed a number of restrictions on capital inflow during January–February 1994. These restrictions included ceilings on external liabilities of commercial banks, a ban on sales of short-term debt instruments to foreigners, restricting ringgit deposits of foreign institutions in non-interest-bearing accounts, prohibiting non-trade-related currency swaps and a new maintenance charge on non-interest-bearing foreign deposits (World Bank, 1996, pp. 67–8; BNM, 1999b, pp. 288–91).

Once speculative pressure subsided and the exchange rate returned to the level of late 1993, BNM gradually removed the controls and eased capital flows, completely lifting all restrictions by August 1994 (World Bank, 1996, pp. 67–8). In June 1995, the finance minister announced a package of incentives to attract foreign fund managers to Malaysia. Trading in financial derivatives on KLSE was started in 1995, with two instruments, namely the KLSE Composite Index Futures and three-month Kuala Lumpur Inter-bank Offer Rate Futures.

The 1993–4 capital control measures appeared drastic and, as in the case of the recent (September 1998) capital control episode (Chapter 6), they led to considerable speculation about capital flight from Malaysia (and from other East Asian countries). In particular, there was widespread concern about a possible future contraction in foreign investment flows to Malaysia, both portfolio investment and FDI. As we will see below, against these gloomy predictions, capital inflows to the country continued to expand at an increasing rate during the ensuing three years.

SURGE OF CAPITAL INFLOWS

The 1990s have seen an accelerated progress towards the liberalization and integration of global financial markets, a process that began in earnest in the

Table 3.1 Net capital flows to developing economies ($ billions), 1984–97

	1984–9[1]	1990–96[1]	1994	1995	1996	1997
Private capital flows	17.8	129.4	133.8	148.2	190.4	139.0
Foreign direct investment	12.2	57.9	76.5	86.5	108.5	126.5
Portfolio investment	4.9	51.1	85.7	22.2	52.7	55.5
Other[2]	0.6	20.4	–28.4	39.5	29.3	–43.0
Official flows	27.2	16.8	10.3	32.1	3.2	–3.3
Change in reserves[3]	5.1	–54.8	–42.3	–67.1	–95.2	–57.8
Total	50.1	91.4	101.8	113.2	98.4	77.9

Notes:
1. Annual average for the period.
2. May include some official flows.
3. Minus implies an increase in national foreign exchange reserves.

Source: Rajan (2000) (based on IMF sources).

1980s. A striking feature of this process of globalization of finance was the growing enthusiasm of hedge funds[6] and other institutional investors for investing in emerging-market economies (Eichengreen and Mussa, 1998; World Bank, 1996). Net capital flows to developing countries reached an all-time high of $190 billion in 1996, more than ten times the average annual flow between 1984 and 1989 (Table 3.1). In this context, capital market liberalization initiatives in the booming Malaysian economy in the early 1990s naturally led to an influx of massive short-term capital flows (Table 3.2).

During the period 1990–96, total net flows to Malaysia amounted to over 12 per cent of GDP, compared to 4.2 per cent in the 1980s. In 1993 this figure hit a historical high of 17 per cent. The private sector was the predominant recipient of foreign capital. Even in the 1980s, when the government and non-finance public enterprises actively mobilized foreign resources from both bond market and international development financial organizations, public sector share of net capital inflows accounted for only about a third of total flows. During 1990–96, this share declined to a mere 1.7 per cent, reflecting the surge of private flows.

The prime mover behind the surge of private capital flows until about 1993 was foreign direct investment (FDI) attracted by a highly favourable domestic investment climate for global production.[7] By the mid-1990s, FDI amounted to more than 4 per cent of GDP, the highest ratio in East Asia after Singapore (Athukorala and Hill, 2000). However, there was a significant compositional shift in private capital inflows from about 1993. While total long-term private

Table 3.2 Malaysia: net capital inflow[1] ($ millions), 1990–97

	1980–89[2]	1990–96[2]	1990	1991	1992	1993	1994	1995	1996	1997
Total capital flows	1 449	8 592	1 790	5 935	8 551	10 291	1 242	7 532	9 432	1 590
GDP	4.9	12.8	4.2	11.7	15.0	16.8	1.7	8.8	9.6	2.2
Composition of total capital flows (%)	100	100	100	100	100	100	100	100	100	100
Official long-term capital	37.9	1.7	–69.8	–6.0	–11.9	2.2	4.7	25.7	2.4	53.0
Federal government	31.7	–10.0	–19.4	0.9	–13.1	–7.2	–26.2	–6.8	–7.0	–19.2
Non-financial public enterprises	6.8	11.8	–50.8	–6.6	1.6	9.8	31.6	32.5	9.1	72.6
Private capital flows	62.1	98.3	169.8	106.0	111.9	97.8	95.3	74.3	97.6	47.0
Corporate investment[3]	61.7	49.5	155.3	98.5	54.5	29.5	59.3	43.7	40.9	164.8
Private short-term capital	0.4	48.8	14.5	7.4	57.3	68.3	36.0	30.6	56.7	–117.8
Portfolio investment	–1.8	37.7	–11.9	–17.3	32.6	58.7	75.2	22.4	28.1	–324.3
Banking sector borrowing[4]	2.2	8.7	26.4	24.7	24.7	9.5	–41.1	6.1	18.4	173.6
Non-bank private borrowing[4,5]	—	2.4	—	—	—	—	1.8	2.1	10.2	32.9

Notes:
1. Net capital flows comprise net direct foreign investment, net portfolio investment (equity and bond flows) and official and private bank borrowings. Changes in national foreign exchange reserves are not included.
2. Annual average.
3. Equity investment, long-terms loans by parent companies and undistributed earnings of foreign-affiliated companies.
4. Borrowing for a period of one year and below.
5. Mostly trade related.

— data not available.

Source: Compiled from Bank Negara Malaysia (1999b) and Bank Negara Malaysia *Monthly Statistical Bulletin*, Kuala Lumpur (various years).

capital flows continued to increase rapidly in absolute terms, their share in total private flows declined significantly as a result of faster growth of short-term private flows. The share of FDI in total inflows declined from an average level of 60 per cent during 1986–90 to about 40 per cent by 1996.

The share of short-term flows surpassed that of FDI in 1992 and hit an all-time high of 62 per cent in 1993. Capital inflow controls implemented by BNM in 1994 (and which lasted until mid-1995) were successful in moderating the surge of short-term flows, but they regained momentum following the lifting of controls, reaching 56 per cent of total inflows in 1996.

Short-term capital inflows to Malaysia were mainly in the form of portfolio capital. They accounted for 45 per cent of total annual capital inflow in 1996, up from 13 per cent in the previous year. Short-term debt of the private sector and banking institutions was low and mainly involved trade-related transactions of the banking system, the bulk of which were hedged (BNM, 1999b, p. 36). In a booming economy there was a natural tendency for the non-financial public enterprises (NFPEs) and private enterprises to increase their access to the international market to meet increased funding requirements. But BNM made use of the legal borrowing limits vigilantly to keep such borrowing within manageable bounds (ibid., p. 38). At the same time, as already noted, the Malaysian Central Bank, unlike its counterparts in Indonesia, Thailand and Korea, continued to maintain prudential regulations on foreign borrowing by the corporate sector. Consequently, there was no significant accumulation of foreign currency borrowing (Table 3.2). Moreover, since the cost of domestic borrowing continued to remain low there was no greater inducement to turn to foreign financial markets. However, it is important to note that short-term bank borrowing did increase significantly in the lead-up to the crisis, accounting for 8.7 per cent of total inflows during 1990–96, compared with 2.2 per cent during 1980–89.

Table 3.3 provides comparative data on the pattern of net foreign capital inflows to East Asia and the five crisis-hit countries in the region during 1990–96. The data clearly bring out the relatively high concentration of inflows to Malaysia in portfolio capital. Portfolio flows accounted for only 20.5 per cent of total flows to the region, compared with 55.5 per cent in Malaysia during this period. Among the five crisis-hit countries, only Korea had a higher share of portfolio investment than Malaysia.[8] In the other three countries this share was less than a quarter of that of Malaysia.

As we will see in Chapter 6, the exceptionally low exposure to short-term foreign debt was a key factor behind Malaysia's unique policy response to the crisis among the five countries. Malaysia had a significantly lower exposure to short-term foreign debt when the crisis broke. It was therefore less severely affected by the debt repayment and servicing burden caused by currency depreciation. However, massive accumulation of portfolio capital did place

Table 3.3 Net capital flows to East Asian developing economies[1] ($ millions)

	1991	1992	1993	1994	1995	1996	1991–96[3]	(%)
East Asia[2]								
Total capital inflows	39 530	21 251	67 157	65 793	94 179	94 129	63 673	100.0
Private capital flows	33 962	15 531	61 205	62 931	90 819	93 217	59 611	93.6
Foreign direct investment	14 072	16 529	42 009	42 181	46 171	52 540	35 584	55.9
Portfolio investment	4 260	12 118	28 190	10 153	19 077	4 495	13 049	20.5
Bank and trade-related lending	15 630	–11 030	–8 930	10 597	25 659	36 182	11 351	17.8
Indonesia								
Total capital inflows	6 648	4 609	6 320	7 076	12 128	12 734	8 253	100.0
Private capital flows	5 365	3 201	4 898	6 899	12 532	14 326	7 870	95.4
Foreign direct investment	1 399	1 536	1 896	2 476	4 649	6 367	3 054	37.0
Portfolio investment	—	—	1 738	1 061	1 415	1 819	1 006	12.2
Bank and trade-related lending	3 965	1 664	1 264	3 361	6 468	6 140	3 810	46.2
Korea								
Total capital inflows	6 766	6 775	3 328	8 425	17 342	23 269	10 984	100.0
Private capital flows	6 472	7 391	5 325	8 705	17 798	23 754	11 574	105.4
Foreign direct investment	–294	–616	–666	–842	–1 825	–1 939	–1 030	–9.4
Portfolio investment	3 236	5 851	10 650	5 055	8 671	11 150	7 436	67.7
Bank and trade-related lending	3 530	2 156	–4 660	4 493	10 953	14 543	5 169	47.1
Malaysia								
Total capital inflows	5 584	6 607	10 799	1 235	7 612	9 416	6 876	100.0
Private capital flows	5 391	6 665	11 185	1 089	7 699	9 516	6 924	100.7

Foreign direct investment	3 995	5 158	5 014	4 140	4 200	5 055	4 594	66.8
Portfolio investment	–708	3 027	9 497	5 485	2 110	3 468	3 813	55.5
Bank and trade-related lending	2 104	1 520	–3 326	–8 536	1 389	993	–976	–14.2
Philippines								
Total capital inflows	2 225	2 066	2 664	3 716	4 449	8 378	3 916	100.0
Private capital flows	727	1 060	1 414	3 204	3 411	8 210	3 004	76.7
Foreign direct investment	545	689	870	1 282	1 335	1 340	1 010	25.8
Portfolio investment	136	53	–54	256	222	–168	74	1.9
Bank and trade-related lending	45	318	598	1 666	1 854	7 037	1 920	49.0
Thailand								
Total capital inflows	11 591	9 808	10 768	12 560	22 529	18 144	14 233	100.0
Private capital flows	10 511	9 696	10 518	12 415	21 352	16 874	13 561	95.3
Foreign direct investment	1 473	1 560	1 377	1 011	1 177	1 633	1 372	9.6
Portfolio investment	—	557	4 007	1 299	3 194	1 089	1 691	11.9
Bank and trade-related lending	9 037	7 579	5 134	10 106	16 981	14 153	10 498	73.8

Notes:

1. Net capital flows comprise net direct foreign investment, net portfolio investment (equity and bond flows) and official and private bank borrowings. Changes in national foreign exchange reserves are not included. For each country, the difference between total and private flows represents net official flows.
2. Sum of the five countries listed in the table, plus China (mainland), Singapore, Taiwan, Hong Kong.
3. Annual average

— data not available.

Source: Compiled from IMF, *World Economic Outlook: Interim Assessment*, December 1997, and Bank Negara Malaysia, *Monthly Statistical Bulletin* (various years) for data on net portfolio capital inflow to Malaysia.

Malaysia in a vulnerable position, as such capital was naturally prone to mass exodus in face of an anticipated currency collapse.

SHARE MARKET BOOM

Increased inflow of foreign portfolio investment fuelled a share market boom in Malaysia from the late 1980s. Market capitalization – total value of all stocks of all national companies listed on the stock exchange – of KLSE as a percentage of GDP increased from a mere 8 per cent in 1985 to 324 per cent in 1996. The composite share price index recorded a staggering ninefold increase between the mid-1980s and mid-1990s (Figure 3.1).

By the mid-1990s, the market capitalization–GDP ratio of Malaysia was the highest among countries in the Asia–Pacific Economic Cooperation (APEC) region, surpassing even the two island economy financial centres of Hong Kong and Singapore (Table 3.4). In terms of annual turnover, KLSE was the

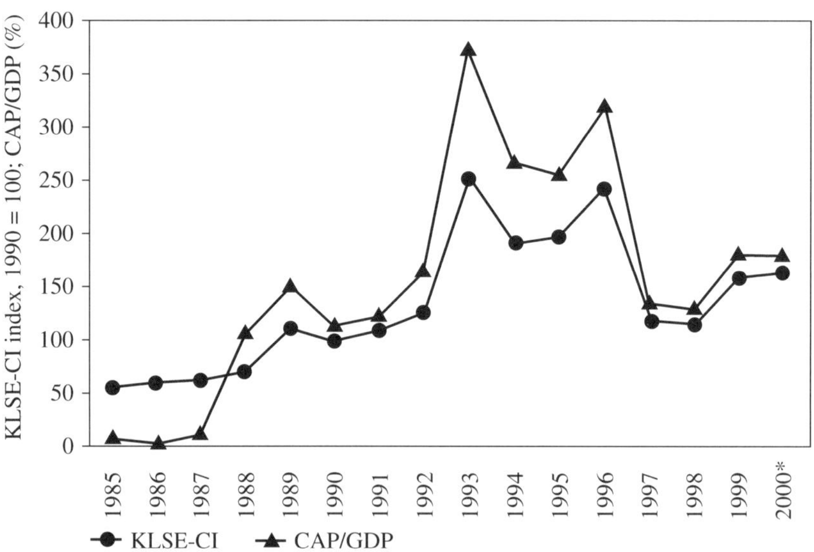

Note: * Data relate to the first three quarters.

Source: BNM (1994, 1999b), updated using BNM website (*www.bnm.gove.my*).

Figure 3.1 Kuala Lumpur Stock Exchange: composite share price index (KLSE-CI, 1990=100) and capitalization–GDP ratio (CAP/GDP) (per cent)

Table 3.4 *Stock market capitalization (% of GDP): East Asia, Australia and the USA*

	Jan. 1990	Jan. 1995	July 2000
Indonesia	—	22.8	33.8
Malaysia	—	248.8	165.0
Korea	54.8	41.2	55.4
Thailand	—	85.6	40.3
China	—	—	8.1
Hong Kong	110.1	218.1	336.7
Taiwan	154.8	84.3	119.9
Singapore	122.9	236.3	261.9
Australia	45.9	61.8	35.6
USA	50.6	62.5	184.5

Note: — Data not available.

Source: Wilson (2000, Table 3) (Goldman Sachs data).

third-largest in the Asia Pacific Region after Tokyo and Hong Kong. There were days when the turnover on the KLSE was higher than that on the New York Stock Exchange (Henderson, 1998, p. 21). As in other East Asian countries, the Malaysian stock market remained heavily concentrated in terms of market capitalization of individual firms. The top ten listed firms accounted for 31 per cent of total turnover by 1997 (Harvey and Roper, 1999, p. 30).

By the mid-1990s, foreign investors accounted for 30–40 per cent of share trading in KLSE (BNM, 1999b, p. 309). However, the actual influence of foreign participation on the expansion and operation of the share market was probably much greater than suggested by this figure. Local investors always followed foreign investors as market leaders.

A striking feature of share trading on the KLSE was the heavy concentration in secondary shares, reflecting the fact that much of the share market boom was driven by speculative share trading rather than new capital mobilization (Table 3.5). During the period 1990–96 new issues accounted for less than 10 per cent, of total turnover, with a period average of 7.7 per cent.

Sectoral composition of new issues (which can reasonably be considered as representative of the distribution of total share trading by sector) exhibited a clear non-traded activity bias. Companies involved in traded-goods sectors accounted for only a third of total new share issues, with the balance coming from companies involved in non-traded activities. In the latter category, the

Table 3.5 *Kuala Lumpur Stock Exchange: turnover, new issues and sectoral composition of new issues, 1990–98*

	1990–96	1990	1991	1992	1993	1994	1995	1996	1997	1998
Total turnover (RM billion)	209.8	29.5	30.1	51.5	387.3	328.1	178.9	463.3	408.6	115.2
New issues	7.7	2.6	2.1	4.4	5.0	10.3	12.2	17.1	19.6	14.2
New issues/turnover (%)	3.7	8.8	7.0	8.5	1.3	3.1	6.8	3.7	4.8	12.3
New issues/gross private capital formation	16.4	6.3	7.1	13.7	12.8	19.9	10.2	22.2	22.8	23.6
Sectoral composition of new issues (%)	100	100	100	100	100	100	100	100	100	100
Traded good sectors	29.7	20.9	30.8	24.2	50.8	37.5	46.2	29.7	25.5	66.5
Agriculture, forestry and fishing	3.3	3.7	3.1	3.8	0.0	6.1	3.0	3.3	2.6	0.0
Mining and quarrying	3.6	0.0	2.3	0.4	0.0	3.5	0.1	3.6	0.0	0.0
Manufacturing	22.9	17.2	25.4	20.1	50.8	27.9	43.1	22.9	22.9	66.5
Non-traded sectors	70.3	79.1	69.2	74.8	49.2	62.5	53.8	70.3	74.5	33.5
Construction	14.6	14.6	17.5	5.6	19.2	18.5	11.6	20.4	18.1	21.7
Electricity, gas and water	4.2	24.9	0.0	32.6	0.0	4.3	0.0	4.2	11.6	0.0
Transport, storage and communication	6.0	6.8	7.2	20.3	0.8	0.4	0.8	6.0	2.1	1.2
Real estate, finance, insurance and business services	24.1	26.8	43.4	14.5	21.9	31.2	32.2	24.1	36.9	10.6
Trade, hotels and restaurants	15.5	6.1	1.1	1.7	7.3	8.1	9.2	15.5	5.8	0.0

Source: Compiled from Bank Negara Malaysia, *Monthly Bulletin of Statistics*, March 1999.

property sector (broadly defined to include construction, finance and business services) accounted for more than two-thirds of new issues. Despite rapid expansion in equity trading, the Malaysian corporate sector continued to rely on internal sources and in particular bank borrowing for much of its expansion (see Chapter 4). The value of new equity issues during the period 1990–96 accounted for only 16 per cent of total private sector capital formation.

As we will see in Chapter 4, share market expansion in Malaysia was also closely linked with the performance of the domestic banking system. Lending for share market activities turned out to be a major source of bank credit expansion in the lead-up to the crisis.

The expansion of the share market in Malaysia was not accompanied by initiatives to redress underlying weaknesses of corporate governance (Gomez and Jomo, 1997; Searle, 1999, Claessens *et al.*, 1999a).[9] Most of the listed companies continued to be tightly controlled by a handful of powerful families. These families often retained majority stakes even in public companies. Family dominance in the corporate sector underpinned close connections between corporate performance and banks and government sources of finance – the essence of what is commonly referred to as 'crony capitalism'.

Manipulation of inter-company share transactions in order to augment profit in privately owned companies (at the expense of listed companies) was a common occurrence in the Malaysian corporate world. In family-controlled companies, large owners had a tendency to direct earnings by their corporations towards private uses rather than towards enhancing the future value of the corporation itself. Such malpractice made share trading vulnerable to financial panic because unconnected (minority) shareholders had every reason to worry about how they would be treated in the event of a market downturn. As we will see in Chapter 5, this weak, opaque system of corporate governance played an important role in contributing to the severity of the crisis in Malaysia.

CONCLUDING REMARKS

In the early 1990s, Malaysia opened up its capital accounts and took a number of initiatives to facilitate short-term capital inflows, motivated by the aspiration to strengthen Kuala Lumpur's role as an international financial centre. Following this policy shift, by the mid-1990s Malaysia had become the depository for a massive volume of volatile foreign capital, in particular portfolio investment. The economy was experiencing a share market bubble in which both foreign investors and domestic banks played a pivotal role. The share market boom had been built on a weak system of corporate governance and much of the share trading was centred on the property sector. In this context, there was a strong *possibility* for a reversal of capital inflows (triggered by a speculative attack on the ringgit, as happened in the second half of 1997) to generate economic collapse through wealth contraction and banking sector instability. However, this possibility would not have been eventuated had it not been for some serious pitfalls on the domestic policy front, which made the economy vulnerable to a speculative attack on the ringgit.

NOTES

1. All other (pre-crisis) high-performing economies in East Asia achieved Article VIII status much later: Indonesia, 7 May 1988 (IMF, 1997); South Korea, 1 November 1988; Thailand, 4 May 1990; Philippines, 8 September 1995.
2. The share market in Malaysia has a history dating back to 1960, when the Malaysia Stock Exchange (MSE) was set up. Following the termination of currency interchangeability with Singapore, MSE was separated into Kuala Lumpur Stock Exchange and Singapore Stock Exchange (SES) in 1973. However, there was no legal restriction on the listing of Malaysian company shares on SES until 2 January 1990.
3. Following the split of KLSE from SES on 2 January 1990, a new 'over the counter market' (which later came to be known as the Central Limit Order Book (CLOB) market) emerged on the same day in Singapore. At the time 133 actively traded Malaysian stocks and six other foreign stocks were listed on this market. The KLSE, however, continued to treat CLOB transactions as unofficial because they were not bound by any corporate disclosure rules or listing requirements.
4. For details on the regulatory framework of Labuan Offshore Financial Centre and the incentives offered, see BNM (1999b, ch. 13).
5. By end of 1996, 47 offshore banks, 4 offshore insurance and reinsurance companies, 13 trust companies, and 3 fund management companies had been incorporated in Labuan.
6. For an interesting account of the operational aspects of hedge funds, with emphasis on the way they made use of their capacity to take temporary control of assets far in excess of their owners' wealth to penetrate emerging market economies, see Krugman (1999b, ch. 7).
7. The Malaysian experience of attracting FDI has been discussed in detail elsewhere (Athukorala and Menon, 1995a).
8. It is important to note that Korea is unique among the five countries, in that it is the only country with net foreign direct investment outflow.
9. Weak corporate governance was a common problem across all crisis-hit countries in Asia (and other emerging market economies). See Claessens *et al.* (1999b) and Harvey and Roper (1999) on the comparative experience.

4. Capital flows and signs of vulnerability[1]

A country succumbs to an international financial crisis[2] when market participants lose confidence in the currency of a particular country and seek to escape assets denominated in that currency as well as other assets whose value might be affected by policy responses induced by a run on the currency. Because investors try to avoid short-term capital losses, the fundamental concern governing their action is the ability of the country to defend the currency in the event of a speculative attack. A situation where there is real room for negative opinion about this ability is referred to as a *state of vulnerability* to a currency crisis (Dornbusch, 1997). It is possible that a currency comes under a speculative attack because of wrong market calculations on the part of the speculators and other arbitrary and unpredictable factors that cause a shift in expectation (Kindleberger, 1996; Obstfeld, 1996). However, a country will be able to shrug off such an attack if it was not in a state of vulnerability, assuming of course that nothing serious will go wrong on the policy front in the panic caused by the unexpected attack.

The purpose of this chapter is to examine how short-term capital inflows interacted with other relevant economic variables in making the Malaysian economy vulnerable to a currency crisis. It also aims to identify possible policy slippage that lay behind the identified sources of vulnerability. To gain perspective, the Malaysian experience is compared with the other four East Asian countries directly affected by the crisis (Thailand, Indonesia, South Korea and the Philippines) and two high-performing countries in the region (Taiwan and Singapore) which experienced only ripple effects of the regional crisis.

VULNERABILITY INDICATORS

There is a sizable body of literature on the vulnerability of a country to a financial crisis.[3] When the Malaysian macroeconomic performance prior to the crisis is closely examined in the light of this literature, there is considerable evidence that Malaysia succumbed to the Thai contagion because its economy had developed considerable vulnerability to a speculative attack.

At least three clear signs of vulnerability were visible in the lead-up to the crisis: inadequacy of foreign exchange reserves to face a speculative attack, considerable deterioration in the quality of financial sector performance (financial fragility) and a significant appreciation of the real exchange rate (suggesting a significant deterioration in international competitiveness). In this section we discuss the underlying theoretical reasoning of these vulnerability indicators and the measurement issues involved. The following section will analyse the state of vulnerability of the Malaysian economy using these indicators.

Reserve Adequacy

Seemingly the most important factor that determines the ability of a country to defend the exchange rate in the face of a speculative attack is the strength of its foreign exchange reserve position. The currency of a country with limited reserves to rely on to meet a sudden outflow of funds naturally becomes an easy target for speculators.

The conventional yardstick used in the literature on balance of payments issues for measuring reserve adequacy is the import-month equivalent of reserves (the ratio of reserves to one month's worth of imports).[4] This measure is not appropriate for the present analysis because 'a run against a currency is rarely associated with an import spree' (Calvo, 1995). What is required is to assess reserve levels in relation to the volume of 'mobile capital' or 'hot money' that can easily flee the country. In other words, the appropriate level of reserves depends on the volume of all short-term liabilities, including portfolio investment.

Some recent studies (for example, Radelet and Sachs, 1998; Goldstein, 1998) have defined mobile capital to cover only short-term bank credit (as reported by the Bank for International Settlements (BIS), based on balance sheets of banks reporting to the BIS). This definition, while obviously more appropriate than the conventional import-month yardstick, tends to understate significantly the volume of mobile capital, particularly because in recent years emerging market economies have experienced large increase in portfolio equity inflows. A country which has accumulated substantial portfolio equity investments held by non-residents needs high reserves, particularly as those shares are held by open-ended funds which may be forced to liquidate their holdings quickly in response to adverse shifts of sentiment. In this study we employ a broad definition of mobile (volatile) capital that covers (a) short-term bank credit (of all banks, not only BIS-reported banks), (b) accumulated portfolio investment, and (c) balances on non-resident bank accounts and trade credits. In the following discussion this measure is referred to as the 'reserve–mobile capital ratio' (R/MC for short).

When capital inflows are reversed, holders of liquid domestic liabilities may also try to convert them into foreign exchange and flee the country. On these grounds, some analysts have opted to measure reserve adequacy by relating foreign reserves to M2, or a broad measure of liquidity money assets (for example, Calvo, 1995; Sachs *et al.*, 1996; Kaminsky *et al.*, 1997; Corsetti *et al.*, 1998). Despite the theoretical possibility, it seems unlikely that growth of M2 in relation to foreign reserves plays an important role in investors' calculation of a speculative run on the currency. In most emerging market economies domestic financial markets are not fully integrated with world financial markets and in practice conversion of money balances into foreign currency is not an option available (or considered) by the majority of such asset holders. Demand for money in the domestic economy is presumably largely independent of speculative factors.

Financial Sector Fragility

If reserves are inadequate to defend the currency, and the country still wants to maintain the exchange rate peg, then raising domestic interest rates becomes an obvious policy tool. An increase in the interest rate is expected to ameliorate the downward pressure on the currency in two ways. First, it helps maintain relative returns to investment in the given country by compensating for potential loss of return due to exchange rate depreciation. Secondly, it may bring about a reduction in domestic absorption (private consumption and investment), which in turn contributes to closing the balance of payments gap created by an initial bout of capital outflow.

A key consideration governing the choice of interest rate policy in the event of a speculative attack is the health of the domestic financial institutions. If the financial institutions have been operating with unsound (fragile) asset portfolios characterized by high non-performing loans, low levels of capital adequacy and other related weaknesses, an interest rate hike is likely to engineer a domestic credit squeeze, bank failure and business bankruptcies leading to economic collapse. Therefore, the more fragile the financial system, the lesser the scope for government to use interest rate policy to defend the currency.

The standard indicators of the health of the banking system are the non-performing loan (NPL) ratio and the capital adequacy ratio. There are, however, serious limitations, both conceptual and in relation to data quality, which make these measures of dubious value for the purpose at hand. First, both measures are backward-looking and, in a context of rapid credit growth, any such historical summary measure is likely to be an inadequate indicator of future performance. Creditors always have the option of arranging credit rollover through their banks. Second, not only in developing countries, but also in developed countries with more efficient bank supervisory mechanisms, these measures are subject to measurement errors, primarily because of ambiguities surrounding the choice among many definitions. Usually, in the face of trouble, banks tend to give themselves the benefit of the doubt, thus making the indicators even more dubious in the context of a crisis (Mishkin, 1997).

Given these considerations, the most widely used indicator of the soundness of the banking system is total outstanding bank credit to the private sector as a ratio of GDP (private sector leverage ratio) (Soros, 1998; Radelet and Sachs, 1998; Sachs *et al.*, 1996; Mishkin, 1996; Backstrom, 1997). This is the main indicator of financial sector fragility used in this study. The underlying hypothesis, which has been amply supported in the context of financial crises in many countries, is that countries with rapid build-up in bank credit (or 'over leveraged' economies) would have more fragile banking systems, a greater quantity of bad loans and therefore greater vulnerability to a crisis. Also rapid build-up of credit in a short period may imply a growing share of lending to less credit-worthy borrowers, and therefore a sign of weakening of the banking system. Ideally, this measure needs to be supplemented by direct measures of the composition of bank lending. As has been repeatedly demonstrated in the world history of financial crises, two economies with the same degree of credit accumulation could have vastly different outcomes in the event of a financial crisis depending on the degree of exposure of the banking system to the property sector (broadly defined to cover real estate, construction and share trading) (Kindleberger, 1996). The property sector, given the high sensitivity of its operation to changes in interest rates and share prices, usually turns out to be the first victim of financial and economic collapse following a speculative attack on the currency (Kindleberger, 1986, 1996; Hall and Ferguson, 1998).

Real Exchange Rate Misalignment

If interest rate policy cannot be used for the above reasons to defend the currency, the required adjustment has to come through a depreciation of the real exchange rate.[5] Real exchange depreciation facilitates a domestic expenditure switch against tradables and towards non-tradables, and thus accommodates the decline in the current account deficit necessitated by capital outflows, without a need for a recession. The required degree of depreciation will be greater the more appreciated the real exchange rate relative to the level compatible with lower capital inflows. For these reasons, in the recent literature on currency crises, persistent appreciation of the real exchange rate (adjusted for fundamentals) has been identified as a major factor in setting the scene for a crisis (Kaminsky *et al.*, 1997, Sachs *et al.*, 1996).

It is important to recognize that a steady, systematic appreciation of the real exchange rate that occurs in line with underlying economic fundamentals is not a problem. If a country borrows to invest and/or attracts significant foreign direct investment, such capital inflow naturally strengthens the real exchange rate – which is the expected effect of an inward transfer. An appreciation can also be a reflection of deep reforms that open up large and lasting opportunities for economic expansion. The 'Balassa–Samuelson' effect – long-term improvement in productivity that normally has a greater price-lowering effect on tradables than on non-tradables – can be another factor. Real appreciation due to these factors should not cause concern about the macroeconomic health of the economy.

A persistent, excessive appreciation (exchange rate misalignment), that is an appreciation which is not justifiable in terms of underlying economic conditions, is what bothers investors and may induce a run on the currency. Such an appreciation implies that the economic fundamentals of the country may not permit the authorities to defend the currency successfully in the event of a speculative attack. In sum, the relevant question is not the actual level of the real exchange rate, but the sustainability of the exchange rate. There is no unique benchmark against which to judge the current level of the real exchange rate. On the other hand, a real exchange rate that is higher than ever before and which continues to appreciate is suspicious, even when major reforms and access to capital markets justify some real appreciation.

In the absence of readily available measures of tradable and non-tradable prices, the real exchange rate has to be proxied by available domestic and world price indices and nominal exchange rates. There is no unique way of constructing a proxy measure. All available proxy measures have been constructed using the general formula:

$$RER_1 = NER\frac{Pw}{Pd},$$

where *NER* denotes the nominal exchange rate (measured in units of domestic currency per unit of foreign currency), *Pw* is an index of foreign prices, and *Pd* is an index of domestic prices. *NER* and *Pw* are weighted averages computed across trading partners, using export, import or total trade (imports plus exports) for assigning weights.[6]

Our preferred proxy measure (denoted RER_1) uses foreign producer prices for *Pw* and domestic consumer prices for *Pd*. Country weights used in constructing *Pw* and *NER* are export shares. Since, by construction, the producer price index is dominated by the prices of tradables and the consumer price index covers both tradables and non-tradables, this index may be a reasonable proxy for the theoretical concept of the real exchange rate.[7]

Previous studies have used two alternative indicators, without making explicit the theoretical reasoning behind the particular measurement choice. One (which we denote RER_2) is the J.P. Morgan index,[8] which measures changes in non-food producer prices in trading partners for *Pw* and wholesale (producer prices) for *Pd*. It is therefore an indicator of the international competitiveness of traded goods produced in the given country. It is not a measure of *internal competitiveness* (the relative profitability of domestic production of tradables compared with non-traded goods and services) which is the real exchange rate concept implied by the theoretical reasoning linking real exchange rate movements with vulnerability to a speculative attack. Wholesale price indices are made up predominantly from traded goods, the prices of which necessarily adjust themselves to exchange rate changes. Thus the true disparity of internal (non-traded good) prices is watered down to a fraction of true value.[9]

The third index (RER_3), which is perhaps the most widely used (particularly in publications of the IMF and the World Bank) uses a trade-weighted index of consumer prices of trading partner countries for *Pw* and an index of consumer prices in the given country for *Pd*. The use of this indicator as a proxy for the theoretical concept of real exchange rate is usually justified on the premise that, under the low inflation conditions that prevail in developed countries (which are generally the major trading partners), producer prices and consumer prices tend to move together. The choice of one over the other is important only in developing countries, which generally tend to experience relatively higher rates of inflation (Edwards, 1989).

Other Indicators

Previous empirical analyses of the causes of currency crises have used a plethora of other indicators, without clearly spelling out the theoretical reasoning behind the anticipated causality. These include the current account deficit, capital inflows, total public debt, government spending – all measured as a percentage of GDP, and the share of short-term debt in total foreign debt and the rate of export growth. In reality, in the context of a currency crisis, most of these variables can be treated as 'leading' indicators whose influences are appropriately captured by one or more of the three vulnerability indicators that we have clearly specified. Some variables are relevant only for various other forms of financial crisis. However, two of these alternative indicators – the current account deficit and the share of short-term debt in total foreign debt – deserve attention, given their frequent use in the popular debate on vulnerability to international financial crises.

The usual reason for using current account deficit (usually measured as a ratio of GDP) as an indicator of vulnerability is that a widening deficit implies dwindling reserves and/or high accumulation of foreign debt, weakening the country's ability to withstand a speculative attack. A rigid interpretation of the current account balance in this manner may, however, be highly misleading; a widening current account deficit could in fact contribute to improvement in the external reserve position of the country and reduce its reliance on foreign debt, provided the net foreign capital that finances the deficit takes the form of productive investment (in particular, FDI in export-oriented product sectors). A more meaningful approach is to focus on specific vulnerability indicators that directly capture the particular aspects of vulnerability that the current account ratio purports to reflect (as discussed above). However, it is not safe to ignore the current account ratio altogether as a completely irrelevant variable, given the market's obsession with it as a key vulnerability indicator. Large and widening current account deficits, regardless of the factors underlying them, can lead to a speculative run on the currency. On these grounds, Summers (1996b, p. 53) comes up with the following rule of thumb: 'Close attention should be paid to any current account deficit of 5% of GDP, particularly if it is financed in a way that could lead to rapid reversal.'[10]

The usual explanation for using the share of short-term debt in total foreign debt as an indicator of vulnerability is as follows (see, for example, Calvo, 1995; Huhne, 1998; Eichengreen, 1999): since short-term foreign debt needs to be rolled over regularly, a country that has accumulated a large stock of short-term debt faces difficulty in defending the currency in the event of a speculative attack. By contrast, so the argument goes, a debt structure characterized by low short-term debt gives a country extra breathing space to turn around its policy in the event of a speculative attack. Such a country does not need continuous large-scale access to the market to service its debt. This indicator, however, suffers from two major limitations. Firstly, official data on the maturity structure of foreign debt, by their very nature, do not capture accumulated portfolio inflows, which in some countries can be an important item of volatile capital. Secondly, in analysing vulnerability what is relevant is the volume of short-term capital in relation to the stock of foreign exchange reserves. A country with a large stock of total foreign debt could well have a small share of short-term debt, yet the magnitude of the latter may be large in relation to the stock of national reserves. For these reasons, this indicator can provide misleading signals as to the state of a country's vulnerability.

SIGNS OF VULNERABILITY

Reserve Adequacy

To recapitulate from Chapter 3, given prudential regulations exercised by Bank Negara Malaysia, there was no massive build-up of short-term foreign borrowing in Malaysia. However, capital market opening and various initiatives to promote Kuala Lumpur as an international financial centre in the early 1990s triggered a significant inflow of portfolio capital. Consequently, the total volume of mobile capital, defined to cover both short-term borrowings and portfolio capital, increased from $6 billion in 1990 to over $50 billion by mid-1997. Over 75 per cent of this increase was accounted for by portfolio capital (Table 4.1). This massive increase in the stock of mobile capital was not matched by an increase in national foreign exchange reserves. Foreign exchange reserves in fact tended to stagnate at around $30 billion from about 1993, following a significant increase during the first three years of the decade. The combined outcome was a rapid erosion of the country's ability to defend the ringgit against a speculative attack (Figure 4.1). Foreign exchange reserves as a ratio of the stock of mobile capital (R/MC) declined from over 150 per cent in the early 1990s to 72 per cent by the end of 1996. This declined further, to 56 per cent by mid-1997, as a result of BNM's attempts to defend the exchange rate of the ringgit in the face of the first round of speculative attack in mid-May (see Chapter 5).

As noted, the most important factor behind the rapid decline in R/MC ratio was accumulation of portfolio inflows. However, stagnation of foreign reserves also played a role. At least three factors contributed to the latter development: rapid import growth fuelled largely by massive construction projects, slowing of export growth (from the latter half of 1995) reflecting adverse demand conditions faced by the electronics exports, and rapid expansion of Malaysian overseas investment.

The last factor was perhaps the most important. With a modest start (less than $10 million) in the early 1990s, total foreign direct investment (FDI) outflow from Malaysia increased to over $3.5 billion (amounting to over 50 per cent of total FDI inflows) by mid-1977. This was predominantly, if not solely, the outcome of an aggressive investment promotion campaign by the Malaysian government, rather than a reflection of local firms expanding their operations overseas as a 'natural' response to global business opportunities. Much of this investment was in construction projects in neighbouring developing countries, Islamic Central Asian republics of the former Soviet Union and South Africa (Athukorala, 1997; Jayasankaran and Thayer, 1996).[11] BNM in its 1996 Annual Report alluded to the fact that outward FDI flows had become a significant net drain on the external reserve position

Table 4.1 Malaysia: end-of-year stock of volatile capital and foreign exchange reserves, 1990–97

	1990	1991	1992	1993	1994	1995	1996	1997[3]
Mobile capital,[1] US$ billion	6.3	6.5	12.4	23.9	27.7	31.9	38.9	50.1
Composition of mobile capital (%)	100	100	100	100	100	100	100	100
Short-term debt[2]	26	40	41	28	20	20	26	28
Banking sector	26	40	41	28	14	14	17	22
Non-bank private	0	0	0	0	6	6	8	6
Portfolio investment	74	60	59	72	80	80	74	72
Foreign exchange reserves, US$ billion	10	11	19	30	26	26	28	28
Reserve–mobile capital ratio (R/MC), %	158	171	149	124	94	80	72	56

Notes:
1. Short-term debt plus portfolio investment.
2. Debt with a tenure of one year and below.
3. First half of the year.

Source: Compiled from Bank Negara Malaysia, *Monthly Statistical Bulletin*, Kuala Lumpur (various issues). The data series on portfolio capital was constructed by accumulating net annual flows from 1980. Data on stocks of other components of mobile capital are readily available in this source.

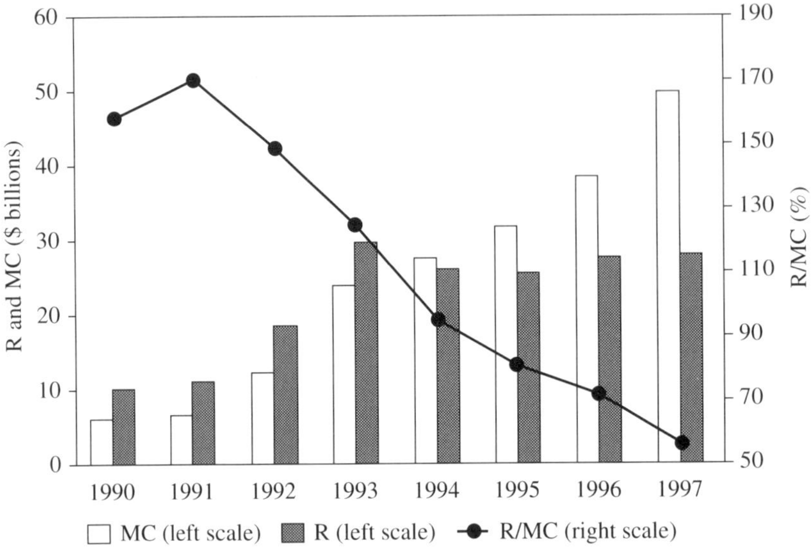

Note: * Mobile capital is defined as the sum of short-term foreign debt and portfolio investment. Data for 1997 are as at end June.

Source: Table 4.1.

*Figure 4.1 Foreign exchange reserves relative to the stock of mobile capital, 1990–97**

of the country as these foreign projects had not yet begun to generate significant return flows.

Malaysia's R/MC ratio is compared with that of the other crisis countries and Taiwan and Singapore in Table 4.2. In the run-up to the crisis, R/MC declined significantly in each of the five crisis countries. The degree of decline in the ratio is most striking for Thailand and Korea. Reserve cover provided for mobile capital in Indonesia, Malaysia and the Philippines were higher compared with Korea and Thailand, but in all these countries there was a persistent deterioration in the degree of reserve cover provided for mobile capital compared with the first half of the 1990s. Interestingly, the two non-crisis countries are clearly distinguishable from their crisis counterparts in terms of the strength of their reserve positions. Taiwan had virtually no accumulated mobile capital in the country. The relatively low R/MC ratio for Singapore compared to Taiwan simply reflects its role as an international banker.[12] By mid-1997, Singapore's total foreign reserves amounted to US$80 billion, the third highest level of national reserves among all East Asian

Table 4.2 Reserve–mobile capital ratio (R/MC) of selected East Asian countries, 1990–97

	1990	1991	1992	1993	1994	1995	1996	1997[1]
Indonesia	125.0	156.3	144.9	106.4	76.9	68.5	70.4	70.5
Korea	116.3	71.9	60.2	49.0	43.7	37.7	29.4	17.8
Malaysia	158.7	170.5	148.7	124.2	94.0	79.9	71.8	55.9
Philippines	416.7	243.9	270.3	208.3	147.1	125.0	93.5	39.5
Thailand	175.4	227.3	169.5	105.3	70.4	61.3	54.1	45.0
Singapore	66.7	93.5	81.3	104.2	126.6	153.8	158.7	101.0
Taiwan	**	**	3333.3	2500.0	1666.7	2000.0	**	**

Notes:
1. First half of the year.
** Stock of mobile capital is negative (cumulative outflow was greater than cumulative inflow).

Source: Athukorala and Warr (1999).

high-performing economies after Hong Kong (US$100) and Taiwan (US$88 billion).[13]

Financial Fragility

The Malaysian banking system has historically been sturdier than its counterparts in most countries in the region. For instance, capital adequacy ratios of Malaysian banks were the highest in Southeast Asia after Singapore. By the mid-1990s, the average capital adequacy ratio for all banks remained over 10 per cent. Some banks even boasted ratios of over 14 per cent, compared with the 8 per cent ratio recommended by the Bank of International Settlement. There was also a requirement that all banks set aside 1 per cent of total outstanding loans as a general provision, in addition to specific provisions made for problem loans (1.5 per cent). Non-performing loans in the banking system fell from 5.5 per cent in 1995 to 3.9 per cent in 1996. Foreign currency exposure of the banking system remained low thanks to the BNM policy of specifying stringent net open positions on foreign borrowing. By mid-1997, the aggregate net open position (foreign currency-denominated bank liabilities net of such assets) of the banking system was less than 5 per cent of total bank liabilities (BIS, 1998).

Despite this apparent soundness in terms of these conventional performance indicators, in the lead-up to the crisis there was a massive accumulation of outstanding domestic credits in the banking system, with a heavy exposure

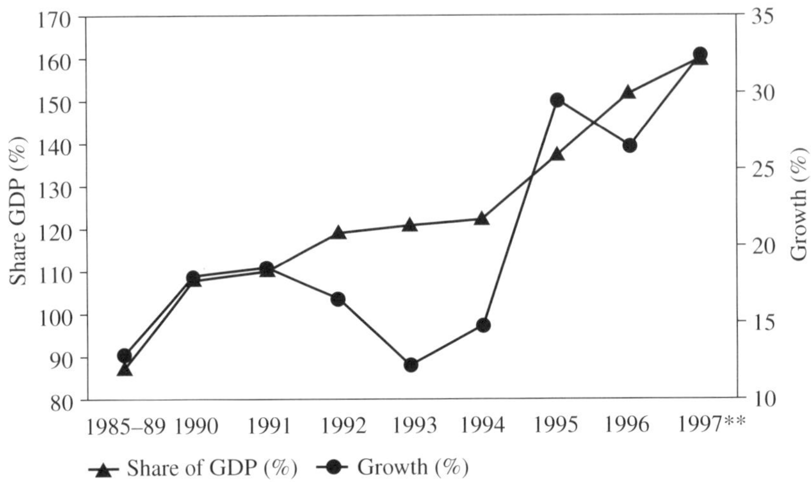

Note: * End of year balance; ** as at end June.

Source: BNM, *Annual Report*, Kuala Lumpur (various issues).

Figure 4.2 Malaysia: bank credit to the private sector as a share of GDP (left scale) and annual growth (right scale), 1985–97*

to the property sector (broadly defined to include share trading and the real estate sector) (Soros, 1998). The rate of growth of bank credit to the private sector (in nominal terms) rose from 8 per cent during 1985–9 to 12 per cent per annum during 1990–94, and to over 28 per cent during 1994–6 (Figure 4.2). Total outstanding credit as a ratio to GDP increased from an average level of 85 per cent during 1985–9 to 120 per cent in 1994 and then to over 160 per cent by mid-1997 when the financial crisis began. As already discussed, a massive credit build-up of this nature invariably limits policy makers' ability to use the interest rate as a policy tool in the event of a speculative attack on the currency.

Beneath the rapid credit growth was a growing concentration of new lending in non-tradable sectors. The share of lending to non-tradable sectors in total outstanding financial sector credit increased from 77 per cent to 80 per cent between 1968–89 and 1996. Within non-tradable sectors, the property sector (broadly defined to cover real estate, share trading and financial services) accounted for over 50 per cent of total credit by 1996. It is believed that this share could be much higher (over 60 per cent) if unclassified loans to conglomerates, which are normally used to finance property, are appropriately taken into account.

Table 4.3 *Ratio of private sector credit to GDP in selected East Asian countries, 1988–97*

	1990	1991	1992	1993	1994	1995	1996	1997[1]
Indonesia	46.9	46.2	45.5	48.9	51.9	53.5	55.4	61.1
Korea	87.5	87.9	95.3	105.2	112.5	117.5	126.5	141.4
Malaysia	123.0	128.9	135.4	147.4	153.1	166.0	175.9	192.5
Philippines	22.3	20.8	25.0	32.0	35.9	45.1	54.2	61.6
Thailand	64.5	67.7	72.2	80.0	91.0	97.6	101.9	116.3
Singapore	95.4	95.7	97.7	96.8	98.4	104.9	110.4	112.9
Taiwan	100.5	109.1	126.4	136.8	146.9	148.9	144.1	145.2

Note: 1. First half of the year.

Source: Athukorala and Warr (1999).

Table 4.3 places Malaysia's credit build-up in comparative perspective. All the five crisis countries experienced credit booms in the lead-up to the crisis. In Malaysia, the degree of private sector leverage, as measured by the ratio of total bank credit to GDP, was the highest of all seven countries.[14] The ratio continued to remain relatively low in Indonesia and the Philippines, but in the lead-up to the crisis its rate of increase was sharper in all five crisis countries compared to Singapore and Taiwan.

Rapid credit growth with a greater concentration of new lending in the property sector occurred in Malaysia in the context of an unprecedented asset price bubble.[15] The increased exposure to the property sector further weakened the financial position of the banks as this lending led to a property glut in the country (Table 4.4). During the period 1994–6, residential property prices in major towns increased by 20–25 per cent per annum, compared with only 4.5–6.4 per cent during 1992–3 (BNM, 1999b, p. 167). These price increases naturally led to a glut in investment in that sector. By the end of 1997, more than 5.8 million square feet of new office space was under construction in the Kuala Lumpur metropolis, on top of 5.6 million square feet of space available at the time (*Far Eastern Economic Review*, 10 April 1998, p. 60). As already discussed in Chapter 3, side-by-side with the real stock boom went a share market boom. The property bubble had direct implications for the banking system because most of the loans to the property sector had been collateralized with property, stocks and shares valued at overinflated prices.

Credit growth also had a significant direct link with the share market boom. The share of lending for share trading in total outstanding bank credit

Table 4.4 *Malaysia: sectoral composition of financial sector credit*[1] *to the private sector (%), 1986–97*

	1986–89	1990	1991	1992	1993	1994	1995	1996	1997
Tradable sectors	22.4	24.4	24.2	23.7	21.9	21.8	22.0	19.8	18.8
Agriculture	5.5	4.9	4.3	3.9	3.1	2.3	2.0	1.9	1.8
Mining and quarrying	1.0	0.9	0.7	0.7	0.5	0.4	0.5	0.3	0.3
Manufacturing	15.9	18.6	19.2	19.1	18.3	19.1	19.5	17.6	16.6
Non-tradable sectors	77.6	75.6	75.8	76.3	78.1	78.2	78.0	80.2	81.2
Electricity	0.1	0.2	0.5	0.5	0.6	1.6	1.5	1.7	1.0
Real estate[2]	36.0	30.3	29.0	29.5	29.6	26.3	25.9	25.7	24.9
Of which private housing	13.6	12.0	12.1	11.9	12.8	11.1	10.0	8.6	7.5
Purchase of share and stocks	1.8	2.1	2.2	1.7	1.9	4.2	3.4	6.6	5.1
Financing, insurance and business services	9.3	9.1	9.3	10.1	11.1	9.8	10.7	12.0	12.1
Transport, storage and communication	1.8	2.1	2.6	2.0	2.1	2.1	2.0	2.4	3.1
General commerce	14.4	12.0	10.9	10.0	9.4	8.9	8.7	8.1	8.7
Consumption credit	5.5	11.1	12.4	11.6	11.6	13.9	13.1	13.8	13.7
Miscellaneous	8.8	8.6	8.7	10.8	11.8	11.4	12.8	9.9	12.6
Total (billion ringgits)	72.7	107.8	131.3	144.0	161.0	184.2	237.8	300.3	392.1

Notes:
1. End-of-year stock of loans and advances of commercial banks and finance companies.
2. Building and construction, purchase of land and private housing.

Sources: Compiled from Bank Negara Malaysia, *Monthly Statistical Bulletin*, March 1999, Tables III-11 and III-12.

increased from less than 2 per cent during 1986–9 to 7 per cent in 1996. As a ratio of GDP, these loans increased from less than 2 per cent in 1990 to over 6 per cent in 1994 and remained at that level until the onset of the crisis in mid-1997. Ogus (2000, p. 45) points to a striking resemblance of the Malaysian situation to the situation in the USA in the lead-up to the Great Depression, where bank lending for stock trading increased from 2 per cent in 1926 to 7 per cent in 1929 (and then collapsed to 2.2 per cent in 1930).

Another important aspect of financial sector performance in Malaysia in the lead-up to the crisis was increased dependence of the corporate sector on bank finance. In 1996, over 61 per cent of total fixed investment in the Malaysian corporate sector was met from bank borrowing. Among the Asian high-performing economies for which data are available only Hong Kong had a higher figure (Table 4.5).

Table 4.5 Sources of business fixed investment in selected East Asian countries (%), 1996

	Hong Kong	Korea	Malaysia	Singapore	Taiwan	Thailand
External sources	97.7	61.4	102.1	58.0	24.8	41.3
Equity	31.3	3.5	21.5	7.7	5.7	6.7
Bond	0.4	9.8	19.5	5.7	0.7	3.5
Bank	66.0	48.1	61.1	44.6	18.4	31.1
Internal sources	2.2	38.6	–2.0	42.0	75.2	58.7
Total fixed investment	100	100	100	100	100	100
As % of GDP	26.8	36.8	29.3	31.4	14.1	31.5

Source: Compiled from Table 5 in Wilson (2000) (Goldman Sachs data).

What Caused Financial Sector Fragility?

Historically, Bank Negara Malaysia had maintained a reputation among the central banks in newly independent countries in the British Commonwealth for strict pursuance of the colonial mould of conservative monetary policy and banking regulation (Bruton, 1993). However, in a context of a credit boom that had government backing at the highest political level (see below), the role of BNM naturally diminished to that of a passive observer of an impending crisis.

From 1992 onwards, BNM attempted on several occasions to use direct credit control, interest rates and moral suasion to calm the credit markets, but all to little avail. Most these measures were subsequently reversed or watered down, reportedly as a result of influence by well-connected lobbies. BNM was eventually allowed to raise the interest rates significantly in 1995 and 1996, but these increases did not have a noticeable impact on credit flows. For instance, although the prime lending rate rose from 7.4 per cent in April 1995 to 9.25 per cent by the end of 1996, the Kuala Lumpur Stock Exchange Composite Index increased by 30 per cent during this period (Ogus, 2000, p. 45). Total bank credit increased by 26 per cent in 1996, compared to 21 per cent in the previous year. The simple lesson was that, in the context of a massive asset price boom, interest rate policy becomes impotent to control credit growth. In this context there was a need for some direct (quantitative) credit restrictions. However, it was only in March 1997 that BNM contemplated introducing some limits on lending to the property sector and share market dealings.

Perhaps the most vivid evidence of a policy conflict between BNM and the prime minister's department emerged from the policy dialogue within the ruling party in the lead-up to the announcement of an IMF-style crisis management package by the then Finance Minister Anwar Ibrahim on 5 December 1997 (see Chapter 5). The following commentary on the cabinet debate of 3 December on the policy package makes interesting reading.

> Anwar presented position papers dating back to 1995 that revealed that both the Finance Minister and the Central Bank had warned of potential economic problems ahead. These included an overheating economy, megaprojects that could strain the country's resources, and unproductive Malaysian investment abroad (*FEER*, 1997b, p. 14).

Direct government influence on bank lending in Malaysia, of course, has a long history, dating back to the launching of the New Economic Policy in 1970, which aimed to restructure business ownership in favour of *Bumiputra* companies (Narayanan, 1996; Searle, 1999). The point made here is that such influence grew out of proportion and turned out to be a major source of macroeconomic instability and financial fragility under Mahathir's 'big push' towards the year 2020.

Finally, it is important to note that the credit boom occurred in a context of growing dominance of local banks (and the diminishing role of foreign banks) in the banking system. Despite significant initiatives in financial liberalization, controls on the entry of foreign banks into the economy remained intact. In the early 1980s, the central bank ruled that only local banks could open new branches. There was also a '60/40 borrowing guideline' for foreign firms operating in Malaysia, stipulating that these firms raise at least 60 per cent of their finances with local banks. With activities of foreign banks artificially frozen, new deposits gravitated towards local banks. By the mid-1990s, foreign banks held about 30 per cent of total bank deposits in the country, down from over 70 per cent in the early 1980s. A greater role for foreign ownership would have provided the banking system with new capital, better management practices and access to foreign lenders in the last resort in the event of a financial crisis (Goldstein, 1998).

Real Exchange Rate Misalignment

For a long period from 1887 to 1967, Malaysia (and Singapore) was in a currency board system, with the Malaysian dollar pegged within a very narrow band to the pound sterling. A newly established central bank (Bank Negara Malaysia) assumed sole currency issuing power in 1967.[16] From then on Malaysia maintained a fixed exchange rate against the US dollar for a little over a decade. In 1978, in response to wide fluctuation of the dollar vis-à-vis other industrial country currencies, Malaysia (following similar moves by Thailand, Korea and Indonesia) switched from the dollar peg to a multi-currency peg basket to stabilize the effective (trade-weighted) exchange rate.

As part of the macroeconomic adjustment package introduced in 1986, greater flexibility was introduced to the basket. BNM's policy was to allow the exchange rate to reflect underlying trends of the economy, while intervening in the foreign exchange market to smooth excessive fluctuation in the exchange rate movements caused by deteriorating short-term capital inflows. These interventions, which mostly took the form of buying foreign exchange, were systematically sterilized in order to avoid domestic inflationary pressure (BNM, 1999b, pp. 36–7; Reisen, 1993).

The real exchange rate index depicted in Figure 4.3 (which was constructed using our preferred formula, RER_1) clearly suggests that this policy was successful in achieving a significant depreciation of the real exchange rate from 1987 to about mid-1993. During this period the real exchange rate depreciated by about 25 per cent, aiding the process of export-oriented industrialization.

The time pattern of *RER*, however, began to reverse from the third quarter of 1993. For the next two years or so it remained stable at a level that reflected about 10 per cent appreciation over the average level for 1987–93. During the next three-and-a-half years preceding the crisis there was a persistent appreciation. The degree of appreciation between 1993 and the first half of 1997 was about 20 per cent. As noted, appreciation of the real exchange rate due to factors related to fundamental structural changes of the economy ('natural' factors) should not cause concern about the macroeconomic health of the economy. As we will argue below, in the Malaysian case there were clear indications that the interaction of exchange rate policy and macroeconomic imbalances, rather than these 'natural' factors, bore much of the responsibility for the recent real exchange rate appreciation.

A real exchange rate appreciation can come through nominal exchange rate appreciation and/or an increase in domestic prices relative to world price.

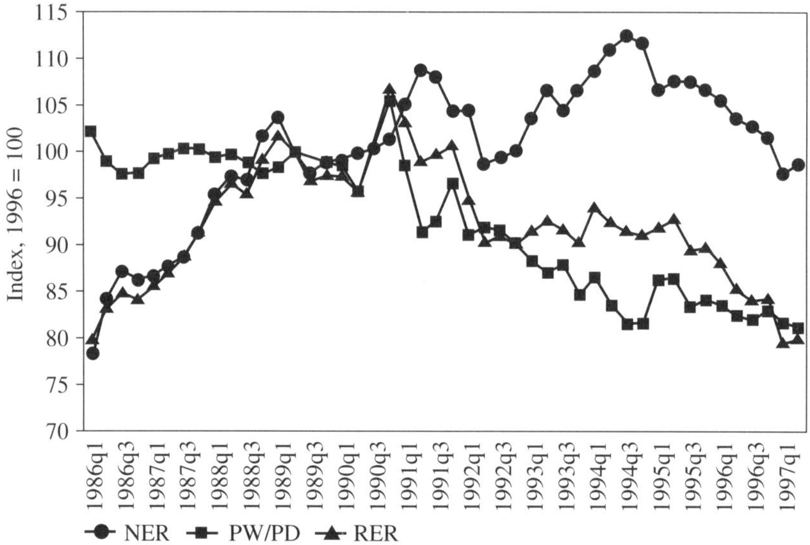

Notes:

NER Export-weighted bilateral exchange rate index of the ten major export destination countries. (An *increase* in NER indicates nominal *depreciation*.)

PW Export-weighted wholesale (producer) price index of the ten major export destination countries.

PD Domestic consumer price index.

RER = [NER*(PW/PD)]*100. (An *increase* in RER indicates *real depreciation*.)

Source: Compiled from IMF, *International Financial Statistics* and *Direction of World Trade* data tapes, and BNM, *Monthly Statistical Bulletin*, Kuala Lumpur.

Figure 4.3 Malaysia: indices of nominal exchange rate (NER), relative price (PW/PD) and real exchange rate (RER)

A comparison of *RER*, *NER* and *PW/PD* series in Figure 4.3 suggests that both these influences underpinned real exchange rate appreciation in Malaysia in the lead-up to the crisis.

To shed light on the factors behind nominal exchange rate appreciation, Figure 4.4 compares trade-weighted nominal exchange rate with the bilateral rates of the ringgit against the dollar (the intervention currency under the quasi-pegged exchange rate system at the time) and the yen. Interestingly, the RM/$ rate remained very stable from about mid-1994 to mid-1997. It appears that by this time BNM had reversed the objective of foreign exchange market intervention away from maintaining a moderate rate of nominal depreciation and in favour of using the exchange rate as an anchor for taming domestic inflation. The volume of foreign exchange reserves of the country, which

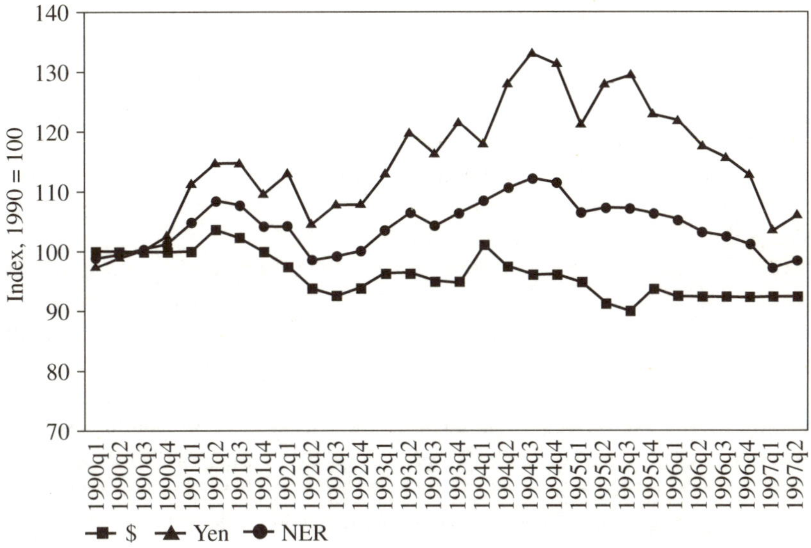

Source: BNM, *Monthly Bulletin of Statistics*, Kuala Lumpur (various issues).

Figure 4.4 Malaysia: bilateral exchange rates against dollar and yen, and trade weighted nominal exchange rate (NER), 1999=100

jumped from $6 billion in 1990 to $30 billion in 1993, declined to an average level of $26 billion during the next three years, despite sizable net capital inflow.[17] While the ringgit remained virtually pegged at a fixed rate to the dollar reflecting this new policy shift, from late 1994 the dollar appreciated significantly against the yen (and also the German mark). Given the high significance of Japan for Malaysia as a trading partner, the outcome was a significant appreciation of the ringgit on a trade-weighted basis, compared to the early 1990s. It is evident from Figure 4.4 that there was a close relationship between the time patterns of the trade-weighted nominal exchange rate (*NER*) and that of the RM/yen rate during the three years before the crisis.[18]

The impact of nominal appreciation on the real exchange rate was compounded by an increase in domestic process relative to world prices (decline in *PW*/*PD*). During 1995–97 the domestic inflation rate (measured by the CPI) was, on average, 2.5 percentage points higher than the average inflation rate in trading partners (measured by the WPI), compared to a near equality in the two rates during 1990–94. Given the highly open trade regime, domestic traded goods prices in Malaysia continued to remain at exchange rate parity (that is, world prices adjusted for the exchange rate). The increase in CPI inflation therefore came predominantly from increases in non-traded goods prices.[19]

The increase in non-traded goods prices was a reflection of mounting domestic demand pressure, emanating largely from a massive construction boom. While the share-market boom and massive domestic credit expansion fuelled a private sector construction boom, the resultant demand pressure was compounded by large public sector infrastructure projects launched as part of the Year 2020 programme (Athukorala, 2001). By the end of 1996, the total estimated cost of various infrastructure projects under construction stood at $62 billion, or 62 per cent of GDP in that year.

Malaysia's real exchange rate behaviour in the lead-up to the crisis is placed in comparative perspectives in Table 4.6. There is clear evidence of continuous appreciation of the real exchange rate in all five crisis countries from about 1992, with the rate of appreciation accelerating in the run-up to the crisis. In the first-half of 1997, real exchange rate of Malaysia had appreciated by about 18 per cent compared to the average level for the period 1988–95, the highest rate of appreciation after Indonesia (22 per cent). The corresponding figures for Thailand, the Philippines and Korea were 15 per cent, 17 per cent and 8 per cent, respectively. Thus, contrary to claims by some authors (such as Kregal, 1998; McKinnon, 1998; Goldstein, 1998), these estimates suggest that these countries were experiencing significant real exchange rate misalignment by the time of the crisis.[20] Interestingly, Taiwan experienced continuous depreciation of its real exchange rate from 1994 to mid-1997.[21]

Table 4.6 Real exchange rate (RER_1)[1] *in Malaysia and selected East Asian countries (1990 = 100), 1991–97*

	1991	1992	1993	1994	1995	1996	1997[2]
RER_1							
Indonesia	96.5	92.7	85.4	80.9	77.5	75.6	68.9
Korea	95.0	95.3	93.3	87.8	82.3	83.5	89.0
Malaysia	96.4	84.4	82.3	79.1	73.9	72.5	70.6
Philippines	90.2	90.6	85.4	83.1	76.9	77.7	72.3
Thailand	94.1	89.5	85.9	80.8	77.1	75.0	74.7
Singapore	93.2	86.7	84.4	77.5	72.6	72.5	73.2
Taiwan	90.1	85.5	86.8	84.1	85.6	91.9	103.1

Notes:
1. Trade-weighted producer price of trading partner countries relative to consumer price of the given country, expressed in a common currency. An increase in the index indicates real exchange rate depreciation.
2. The first half of the year.

Source: Athukorala and Warr (1999).

Other Factors

Do the current account ratio and the short-term debt ratio, which are widely used in the currency crisis literature, add additional information about vulnerability to a currency crisis over and above the indicators we have already discussed? In other words, do they reveal better commonality among the crisis countries in the lead-up to the crisis?

Malaysia recorded current account ratios above the so-called 'critical level' of 5 per cent in only three of the seven years preceding the crisis. More importantly, the current account deficit significantly *narrowed* in 1996 compared with the previous year. A similar pattern is revealed by the data for the Philippines. In Thailand, the ratio was notably high (at 8 per cent) among the five countries in 1995 and 1996, but it did not make a significant deviation from the current account poisition of the country in the early years of the decade. In Indonesia and Korea, the ratios were below 5 per cent in all years. The only clear pattern one can observe in Table 4.7 is that both non-crisis countries (Singapore and Taiwan) had current account surpluses in all years while the crisis countries were overall deficit countries.

Table 4.7 Current account balance in Malaysia and selected East Asian countries (% of GDP), 1990–97

	1990	1991	1992	1993	1994	1995	1996	1997
Indonesia	–2.8	–3.7	–2.2	–1.3	–1.6	–3.2	–3.4	–2.2
Korea	–0.9	–2.8	–1.2	0.3	–1.0	–1.9	–4.8	–1.9
Malaysia	–2.0	–8.7	–3.7	–4.7	–6.3	–8.4	–4.9	–4.9
Philippines	–6.1	–2.3	–1.9	–5.6	–4.6	–2.7	–4.8	–5.2
Thailand	–8.5	–7.7	–5.7	–5.1	–5.6	–8.1	–8.1	–1.9
Singapore	8.3	11.3	11.4	7.6	16.1	16.8	15.7	15.4
Taiwan	4.7	4.4	1.7	1.6	1.7	1.6	3.5	2.4

Source: Compiled from *International Financial Statistics Yearbook 1998*, Washington, DC: IMF.

In terms of short-term debt build-up, too, one cannot observe a clear commonality among the five crisis-hit countries during the years leading up to the crisis (Table 4.8). Among these countries, inter-country differences in terms of this measure are not consistent with what we observe in terms of the R/MC, which is a more comprehensive indicator of a country's ability to defend the currency against a speculative attack. In the lead-up to the crisis,

Table 4.8 Share of short-term debt in total external debt in Malaysia and selected Asian countries, 1990–97

	1990	1991	1992	1993	1994	1995	1996	1997[1]
Indonesia	15.9	18.3	20.5	20.2	18.1	20.9	25.1	32.2
Korea	30.9	28.2	27.0	25.8	41.3	47.5	49.1	49.4
Malaysia	10.5	12.6	23.5	25.0	19.4	19.1	26.2	31.1
Philippines	14.6	15.3	15.9	14.0	14.3	13.3	19.3	22.3
Thailand	29.5	33.1	35.2	43.0	44.5	49.4	41.4	46.2

Notes:
1. First half of the year.
2. Data are not available for Singapore and Taiwan. In these countries external short-term borrowings were presumably zero or negligible during this period.

Source: Compiled from World Bank, *World Development Indicators* data tapes.

Indonesia and Malaysia had much lower short-term debt shares than Korea and Thailand.

CONCLUDING REMARKS

The analysis in this chapter has yielded convincing evidence that, in the lead-up to the crisis, the Malaysian economy had developed considerable vulnerability to a speculative attack on the ringgit. Rapid build-up of mobile capital in relation to the level of international reserves, deterioration in the health of the financial system and a significant appreciation of the real exchange rate were the main signs of Malaysia's vulnerability. In terms of these indicators there was a remarkable similarity between Malaysia and the other four countries.

A state of vulnerability by itself does not give rise to a financial crisis. There needs to be a certain disturbance (a trigger) that will push a vulnerable situation into an actual collapse. For Malaysia (and also for Indonesia, the Philippines and Korea) the trigger was the Thai contagion: investor panic spreading from Thailand.[22] Following the Bank of Thailand's unexpected decision on 2 July 1997 to abandon the cherished exchange rate peg, the baht collapsed dramatically relative to other currencies. In response to this 'wake-up call', fund managers around the globe began to test the strength of the currencies of other high-performing countries in the region, which they had until then treated as equals in the same growth club. Malaysia and other countries, which had developed considerable vulnerability, succumbed to these speculative attacks while others, in particular Taiwan and Singapore, given their sound economic conditions, were able to shrug them off.

NOTES

1. This chapter draws heavily on Athukorala and Warr (1999).
2. In this book the terms 'international financial crisis' and 'currency crisis' are used interchangeably to refer to *speculative attacks on national currencies that bring about financial instability and economic collapse.*
3. See Edwards (1999b), Kaminsky *et al.* (1997) and Dornbusch *et al.* (1995) for comprehensive surveys.
4. The old rule of thumb here is that official foreign exchange reserves should be equivalent to at least three months' worth of imports. This rule originated in the days of the old Bretton Woods system when, given the combination of fixed exchange rates and controls on flow of capital, the worst situation that could be imagined relating to balance of payments management was that a country would lose its trade credit, worth roughly three months of imports (Huhne, 1998, p. 63).
5. The real exchange rate is the relative price of traded to non-traded goods.
6. Export weights are preferred here to import trade weights because they relate to the competitive position of export industries. Import weights do not necessarily indicate the competitive position of import-competing industries and 'trade' weights – obtained by adding imports to exports for each commodity group – seem to have no economic basis at all.
7. For an analysis of the accuracy of this approximation, see Warr (1986).
8. This index is reported on a regular basis (for a number of countries including Malaysia) on the J.P. Morgan website <*http://www.jpmorgan.com.*
9. For an interesting exposition of this limitation of international price comparison based on wholesale price indices (made in the context of the debate on the UK's return to the gold standard at a seemingly appreciated gold parity compared to the prewar level) see Keynes (1925, p. 249).
10. For a penetrating analysis of the limitations of the current account ratio as a crisis indicator, with extensive reference to the related literature, see Edwards (1999b, pp. 295–305).
11. Prime Minister Mahathir was directly involved in the overseas investment drive through legions of Malaysian business leaders to various countries. The news media often reported that he made use of his active role in promoting 'South–South' cooperation to tip the scale towards Malaysian companies in international bids for construction projects in developing countries.
12. Balances in non-resident bank deposits are classified as short-term debt in balance of payments accounts.
13. These figures are from IMF, *International Financial Statistics Yearbook 1998* and Council of Economic Planning and Development, Republic of China, *Taiwan Statistical Data Book 1998.*
14. In his highly-publicized interchange with the Malaysian Prime Minister Dr Mahathir, the financier George Soros pointed to massive private sector credit accumulation as the main source of vulnerability of the Malaysia economy (Athukorala, 1998a, p. 927).
15. On the experience of the other Asian crisis countries see Goldstein (1998), Harvey and Roper (1999) and Rajan (2000). Among these countries, Indonesia and Thailand also experienced massive property booms fuelled by bank financing.
16. A currency interchangeability agreement with Singapore, which assured 100 per cent convertibility between the two currencies, was maintained until 1973.
17. Annual net capital inflows did moderate after 1993, but remained sizable (around an average level of $6 billion up to the onset of the crisis).

18. Using a model of exchange rate determination derived in the context of the monetary approach to the exchange rate behaviour, Husted and MacDonald (1999) find that, among the currencies of the crisis-hit countries, the Malaysian ringgit experienced the highest rate of appreciation (16 per cent) in 1996 against the yen.
19. For instance, during 1994–6 the annual rate of inflation measured by the WPI (which is dominated by traded goods) was a mere 1.1 per cent, compared to a CPI-based inflation rate of 4.5 per cent.
20. Athukorala and Warr (1999) have examined the sensitivity of the result of this inter-country comparison to the use of the other two real exchange rate proxies (RER_2 and RER_3). This comparative analysis convincingly points to the importance of selecting a real exchange rate proxy on the basis of sound theoretical reasoning. Conflicting results reported in various studies may reflect insufficient attention paid to relevant theoretical consideration in choosing a particular exchange rate proxy.
21. The degree of real exchange rate appreciation experienced by Singapore in the lead-up to the crises was similar in magnitude to that of Malaysia. Presumably, the significant depreciation of the yen against the US dollar during this period exerted a considerable pressure of real exchange rate appreciation across those countries in the region, which continued to use the US dollar as the dominant intervention currency in their pegged exchange rate systems. Singapore is, however, unique among these countries, given the persistent appreciation of the real exchange rate throughout the period from 1990 (and even before), reflecting perhaps rapid structural adjustment in the economy.
22. What triggered the crisis in Thailand remains a moot point. Miller convincingly argues that the trigger was the sudden revelation that much (around \$30 billion) of Thailand's official reserves (\$37 billion reserves) had been locked in long positions in the forward market (Miller, 1998, p. 356). For other explanations, see Rajan (2000).

5. Onset of the crisis, policy slippage and economic collapse

For over five years prior to the onset of the recent currency crisis, the exchange rate of the ringgit varied in the narrow range of 2.36 to 2.51 ringgit per US dollar. When the Thai baht came under heavy speculative attack in mid-May 1997, the ringgit also experienced heavy selling pressure. BNM responded with massive foreign exchange market intervention; it sold close to $1.5 billion to prop up the ringgit. Speculative attacks intensified following the collapse of the Thai baht on 2 July. BNM held the ringgit firmly through continued market intervention for another week and then gave way to market forces on 14 July by floating the currency. With the ability to defend the currency dramatically reduced, and without any indication as to the depth of the impending crisis, letting the exchange rate float was indeed the only sensible policy.

CURRENCY SLIDE AND SHARE MARKET COLLAPSE

Between the first week of July 1997 and 7 January 1998, when the currency slide hit bottom (RM4.88/$), the ringgit depreciated against the dollar by almost 50 per cent (Figure 5.1). After showing some signs of stability during February and March, the exchange rate continued to deteriorate with wider swings in the following months (until it was fixed at the rate of RM3.80/$). This contrasted with the experience of Thailand and Korea, where from March onwards currencies showed signs of stabilizing at higher levels.

In a proximate sense, reversal of foreign capital was the key factor behind the exchange rate collapse. In a significant departure from the experiences of the other four East Asian crisis countries (Thailand, Indonesia, Korea and the Philippines), in Malaysia it was portfolio capital that accounted for virtually all of this reversal (Figure 5.2).[1] Net quarterly flow of portfolio capital turned negative in the second quarter of 1997 for the first time since 1991 and total net outflow in the first three-quarters of the year amounted to over US$11 billion. By contrast, net short-term bank borrowing *increased* by about US$3 billion during this period.[2] Reflecting the massive reversal of portfolio capital flows, the share market tumbled in tandem with the exchange rate collapse.

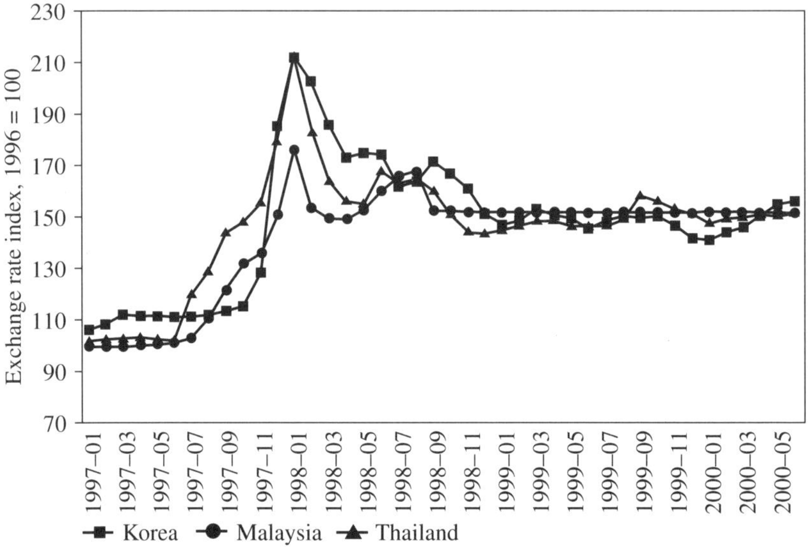

Source: Asia Recovery Information Centre Data Base, Asian Development Bank (http://aric.adb.org).

Figure 5.1 Exchange rates of Korea, Malaysia and Thailand (units of local currency per US$, 1996=100), January 1997–June 2000

Malaysia experienced the biggest stock market plunge among the five crisis countries in East Asia (Athukorala, 1998b). By the end of 1997, the all ordinary index of the Kuala Lumpur Stock Exchange (KLSE) had fallen by over 50 per cent from its pre-crisis level (Figure 5.3), whipping off almost $225 billion of share values. The price–earnings (P/E) ratio of KLSE declined from 22.9 to 11.3 over this period.

During the economic boom in the lead-up to the crisis, foreign investors were injecting funds into Malaysian firms, despite their high debt ratios and murky inter-company relationships, which would not have been acceptable under normal circumstances. The extent of subsequent portfolio capital outflows owed much to the realization that much of the capital should not have been committed in the first place. When the foreign participants started pulling out to avoid currency risk following the onset of the currency crisis in mid-1997, the local players panicked. On the basis of past experience, the minority shareholders were naturally concerned that they might be the hardest hit in troubled times (*The Economist*, 1997a).

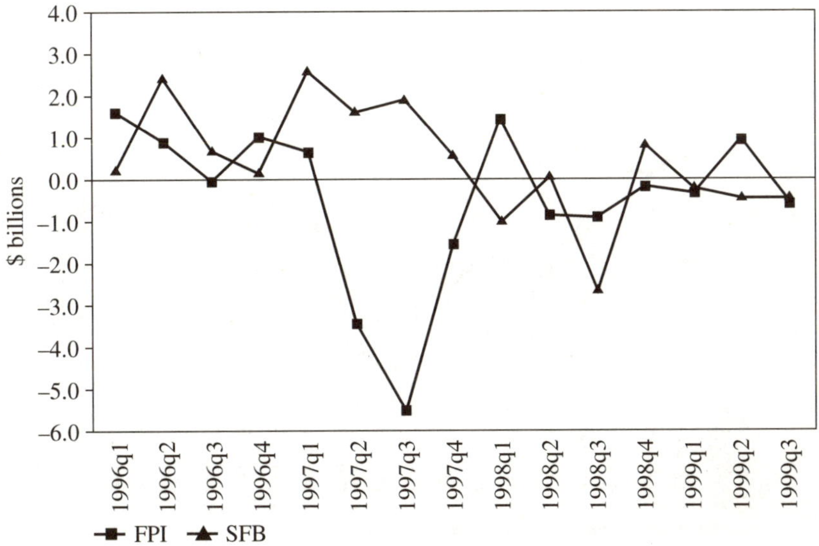

Source: Data compiled from Bank Negara Malaysia, *Monthly Statistical Bulletin* (various issues).

Figure 5.2 Malaysia: foreign portfolio investment (FPI) and short-term foreign borrowing (SFB) (net flows, US$ billions), 1996Q1–1999Q3

MUDDLING THROUGH

As noted, Malaysia, unlike Thailand, Indonesia and Korea, succumbed to the crisis with low foreign debt exposure of its banking system (see Chapter 3). For this reason, the Malaysian policy makers were able to 'muddle through' without an IMF-sponsored rescue package.

The initial response of the Malaysian government to the outbreak of the currency crisis was one of denial. Given the perceived soundness of economic fundamentals, Prime Minister Mahathir's immediate reaction was to pounce on the villains: currency speculators. By implicating the American financier George Soros (a Jew of Hungarian origin) in the speculative attack, he complained about a Jewish conspiracy to jeopardize the Malaysian miracle. At the IMF and World Bank annual meetings in Hong Kong in late September 1997, Dr Mahathir stated that currency trading (beyond what is required to finance trade) was 'unnecessary, unproductive and immoral', and that 'it should be made illegal'.[3] Dr Mahathir continued his attack on speculators in domestic and international forums, including the Annual Asia–Pacific

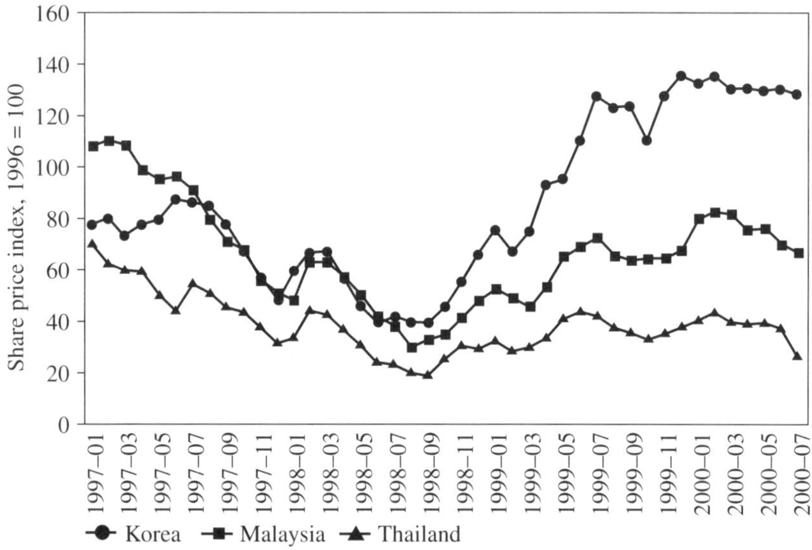

Source: Asia Recovery Information Centre Data Base, Asian Development Bank (*http://aric.adb.org*).

Figure 5.3 Monthly share price indices of Korea, Malaysia and Thailand, January 1997–July 2000

Economic Cooperation (APEC) summit on 18 November in Vancouver and the Commonwealth Heads of Government Meeting in Birmingham in the same month. Almost every attack by Dr Mahathir against his perceived enemies precipitated a further sliding of the ringgit.

Even more damaging to investor confidence than the prime minister's attacks on speculators were several initiatives to intervene directly in share market operation with a view to punishing speculators (Hale, 1997). On 28 August, the KLSE banned the short selling of 100 blue-chip stocks and rules were introduced to discourage the sale of stocks: sellers were required to deliver physical share certificates to their brokers before selling and the settlement period was reduced from five to two days. On 3 September, the prime minister unveiled a plan to use funds from the Employees Provident Fund (EPF) to prop up share prices by buying stocks from Malaysian shareholders – but not foreigners – at a premium above prevailing prices. These moves backfired, triggering a massive sell-off of stocks in KLSE and undermining sentiment on other regional bourses. Ironically, the share purchases sponsored by the government were seen by market participants, both local and foreign, as an opportunity to get rid of Malaysian shares, rather than a reason for holding on to them.

There was some retreat from this 'unorthodox' policy posture during the ensuing months as the crisis deepened. The ban on short selling was lifted in early September. In the same month, the government announced the postponement of some grandiose infrastructure projects amounting to about $10 billion of investment commitments. The Budget for 1998 unveiled on 17 October contained some measures to reduce the current account deficit through selective import duties and a 'buy Malaysia' campaign. However, the government failed to come up with a coherent programme of reforms to deal with the crisis.

After a period of policy indifference of over five months, a major policy package was announced by the then Finance Minister Anwar on 5 December 1997. The key elements of the package included cutting government spending by 18 per cent, postponing indefinitely all public sector investment projects which were still in the pipeline, stopping new overseas investment by Malaysian firms, freezing new share issues and company restructuring, and cutting salaries of government ministers by 10 per cent. With these measures, the previous Budget forecast of economic growth (7 per cent) was lowered to 4 per cent–5 per cent. BNM increased its three-month intervention rate from 7.55 per cent to 8.7 per cent. It reduced the period in arrears (default period) for classifying a loan as non-performing by banking institutions from six months to three months, with a view to strengthening prudential supervision. To complement this policy package, BNM increased the inter-bank lending rate (BNM's policy rate) from the pre-crisis level of 7.6 per cent to 8.7 per cent in December 1997, and to 10 per cent in January and 11 per cent in February 1998.

The 5 December policy package undoubtedly marked the most important economic policy shift in the decade. The news media labelled the package, coupled with the subsequent monetary tightening by BNM, as 'IMF policy without IMF' (*FEER*, 1997b). However, the government quickly backtracked from this policy stance, compounding policy uncertainty.

The state of policy paralysis was widely ascribed by the news media to a widening policy rift between the prime minister and the finance minister. From the onset of the crisis there was an apparent conflict between Dr Mahathir and his deputy and finance minister (and heir apparent), Anwar Ibrahim, over how to manage the crisis. Following Mahathir's attack on speculators at the IMF–World Bank meeting in Hong Kong, Anwar acted quickly to assure the international investment community that the government would not introduce capital controls. This suggested a policy disagreement at the top level for the first time. Subsequently, measures to tame speculators were announced in September by Dr Mahathir alone, and Anwar never expressed a view on them. The December 1997 austerity package was announced by Anwar, and Mahathir openly tried to dissociate himself from its orthodox policy posture. In presenting the policy package, Anwar quoted from position papers dating back to 1995 to support the view that the financial crisis was not simply a sporadic speculative attack (as widely alleged by Mahathir), but both the central bank and the finance ministry had repeatedly warned about impending economic problems. In all these instances the international news media speculated on a possible rift between the two ministers. Many observers are of the view that this apparent conflict contributed to policy indecisiveness in tackling the crisis, and reduced the effectiveness of whatever policy measures were taken by increasing the 'political risk premium'.[4]

A National Economic Action Council (NEAC) was established on 7 January 1998 to act as a consultative body to the cabinet 'to chart its own course of action, instead of following IMF's prescription' (Government of Malaysia, 1999, p. 9).[5] The NEAC was chaired by the prime minister himself, with Daim Zainuddin, a confidant of Dr Mahathir and former finance minister, as the executive director. The media interpreted this step as a calculated plan to sideline Anwar Ibrahim from the policy scene. That day, the ringgit touched a historic intra-day low of 4.88/$.

Over the next eight months the contractionary monetary and fiscal policies introduced in late 1997 were reversed in an ad hoc manner, rather than as part of a crisis management package. BNM *reduced* the statutory reserve requirement (SRR) from 13.5 per cent to 10 per cent in February 1998 and to 8 per cent in July 1998. The bank justified this as a necessary step to 'avoid a recession–deflation spiral' (BNM, 1999a, p. 4) in a context where rapid contraction in economic activity had begun to be reflected in a massive build-up of non-performing loans in the banking system and corporate failures. The three-month inter-bank intervention rate was reduced in three steps from 11 per cent to 9.5 per cent in August. Proposed cuts in government expenditure were restored and a number of large projects that had been halted were reactivated. By mid-1998, fiscal policy turned out to be more expansionary to compensate for the slack in private sector demand. The government announced in July a fiscal stimulus package of RM7 billion. An Infrastructure Fund worth RM5 billion was also established.

The National Economic Recovery Plan (NERP) prepared by the National Economic Action Council was launched on 23 July 1998 (NEAC, 1998). By and large, NERP took the form of a *policy blueprint* rather than a concrete action plan for managing the crisis. It made a case, in broader terms, for easing of fiscal and monetary polices and expediting reforms to revitalize the financial sector, but failed to come up with a concrete programme of action for restoring macroeconomic stability and investor confidence.

Beginning in May 1998, the Malaysian authorities set up an institutional framework for recapitalizing the troubled banks and resolving mounting corporate distress. As the first step, an asset management company (*Pengurusan Danaharta Nasional Berhad*, henceforth referred to as *Danaharta*) was set up to acquire and manage NPLs from banks. This was followed by the establishment in July of a banking and corporate recapitalization company (*Danamodal Nasional Berhad*, henceforth referred to as *Danamodal*) as a special agency with the purpose of recapitalizing those financial institutions whose capital adequacy ratio had fallen bellow 9 per cent. Finally, to complement the roles of *Danaharta* and *Danamodal*, a Corporate Debt Restructuring Committee (CDRC, a joint public and private sector steering committee) was established in August to facilitate the restructuring of corporate debts through out-of-court settlement between debtors and creditors.[6] The three institutions taken together provided a systematic institutional framework (apparently designed with the involvement of reputable international consultancy firms) for addressing the bad debt problem of the financial system and related corporate distress, which had already begun to emerge as major constraints on the recovery process. This initiative was widely hailed by the financial press as an important step in the right direction,[7] but difficulties in obtaining the required funds precluded concrete policy action by these institutions. Thus BNM had to continue to cushion the banking sector and debt-ridden companies against the liquidity squeeze caused by the share market crash and capital outflow by keeping a lid on interest rates and injecting liquidity into the system by printing money.

ECONOMIC COLLAPSE

By August 1998, the economy was in recession and there were no signs of achieving currency and share price stability. According to national account estimates announced in March 1998, the economy had contracted by 2.8 per cent (on an year-on-year basis) in the final quarter of 1997 (for the first time in 12 years), bringing the growth rate for the full year down to 7.5 per cent compared to 8.5 per cent in the previous year. National accounts released in the last week of August revealed a further contraction of output by 6.8 per cent, confirming that the economy was in deep recession.

Total employment declined by 3.1 per cent in 1998, compared to an average growth rate of 4.5 per cent for the previous five years. The largest employment contraction was in the construction sector (16.9 per cent), with manufacturing recording a 3.6 per cent decline. The number of retrenchments in domestic manufacturing jumped from 19 000 in 1997 to over 83 000 in 1998. The unemployment rate increased from 2.6 per cent in 1996 to 3.9 per cent in 1998. (The increase in unemployment would have been much sharper had it not been for the cushioning effect of the repatriation of a large number of foreign workers following the onset of the crisis.)[8]

The inflation rate (measured by the consumer price index (CPI)) peaked at 6.2 per cent in June, surpassing the previous peak of 5.3 per cent recorded in 1991. Given the crisis-generated excess capacity in the economy and signs of increase in unemployment, the increase in the rate of inflation was commonly interpreted as a reflection of the excessive depreciation of exchange rate (BNM, 1999b, p. 165; Ariff, 1999).

The combined outcome of economic collapse and the property market crash was a massive increase in non-performing loans in the banking system. This situation was further aggravated by a 'flight to quality' of deposits from smaller to large, well-managed banks from the fourth quarter of 1997. The competition for funds by the affected institutions resulted in a sharp increase in lending rates (exceeding 20 per cent in early 1998) in the banking sector as a whole. These higher lending rates in turn weakened banks' balance sheets by increasing the level of non-performing loans (BNM, 1999b, p. 175).

According to BNM data, the proportion of non-performing loans in total bank assets increased from about 2 per cent in July to 3.6 per cent in December 1997 and then to 11.8 per cent in July 1998. Market analysts believed, however, that the problem was much more severe than the official figures suggested. This was because many companies had begun to roll over debt as part of their survival strategy. Independent estimates of the non-performing loan ratio ranged from 25 per cent to 30 per cent by mid-1998 (Hiebert, 1998; *Financial Times*, 1998; Soros, 1998, p. 144).

Banks, because of the deterioration of balance sheets and/or because of over-cautiousness in an uncertain financial environment, tended to focus on loan recovery rather than issuing new loans. Consequently, growth of net outstanding bank loans (in nominal terms) declined from over 26 per cent per annum during the five years prior to the crisis to 9 per cent during the year ending July 1998. Annual rate of growth of money supply (M3) declined from 18.5 per cent at the end of 1997 to 4.4 per cent by August 1998.

Credit contraction began to have an impact on domestic consumption and investment. Falling asset prices exerted pressure on debtors to sell assets, leading to further decline in asset prices. To make matters worse, the much hoped-for export-led recovery was not on the horizon, despite massive improvement in competitiveness achieved through currency depreciation. Business confidence of manufactures as measured by the Business Confidence Index (BCI) of the Malaysian Institute of Economic Research (MIER) had dipped sharply for three consecutive quarters, starting in the second quarter of 1997. MIER's consumer sentiments index (CSI) released in July 1998 was at an all-time low for the decade (Figure 5.4).

The weaker investor confidence resulting from rapid depreciation of the ringgit and uncertainty in the financial market led to continued liquidation of

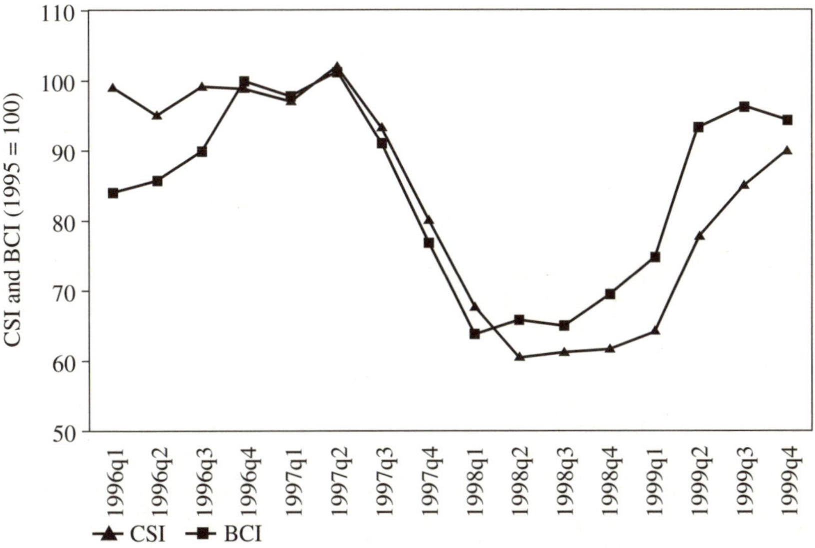

Source: Malaysian Institute of Economic Research, *Consumer Sentiments Quarterly Report* and *Business Confidence Quarterly Report* (various issues), Kuala Lumpur. The original indices have been recast to a common 1995 base for easy comparison.

Figure 5.4 Indices of Consumer Sentiment (CSI) and Business Confidence (BCI), 1996Q1–1999Q4 (1995 = 100)

shares by foreigners. This in turn brought external reserves of the country to alarmingly low levels, despite massive import contraction in a depressed economy. Worsening business confidence led to a large outflow of short-term capital. Total net outflows during the first two quarters of 1998 amounted to \$3.5 million. Because of these capital outflows, the recession-induced current account surplus did not result in an improvement in the foreign reserve position of the country (Table 5.1). This was in contrast to the experience of the four IMF-programme countries (Thailand, Indonesia, the Philippines and Korea) where widening current account surpluses boosted international reserves, preventing further exchange rate collapse (World Bank, 1998).

A striking feature of capital flights from Malaysia from about early 1998 was that they largely took the form of ringgit (rather than foreign currency) flowing into Singapore.[9] As much as 25 to 35 billion ringgit (\$6.3–8.8 billion) had ended up in Singapore at the height of the crisis in mid-1998 (Ariff, 1999; Tripathi *et al.*, 1998; IMF, 1999b). This amounted to 40 to 60 per cent of the total domestic supply of narrow money (M1) and 9 to 11 per cent of broad money (M2) in Malaysia. These flows were triggered by very attractive money

Table 5.1 Malaysia: balance of payments (US$ millions), 1997–9

	1997	1998Q1	1998Q2	1998Q3	1998Q4	1999Q1	1999Q2	1999Q3	1999Q4
Exports	77 829	17 330	17 422	19 135	19 508	18 087	20 419	22 232	23 193
Imports	73 716	14 446	13 689	13 756	13 564	13 142	14 814	15 824	17 379
Trade balance	4 034	2 883	3 733	5 379	5 943	4 945	5 605	6 162	5 814
Services and transfers (net)	–9 071	–1 240	–1 536	–2 079	–2 482	–2 104	–2 350	–2 464	2 997
Current account	–5 037	1 643	2 197	3 300	3 461	2 841	3 247	3 698	2 817
Long-term capital (net)	6 764	372	785	–667	593	84	972	594	111
Basic balance	1 727	2 015	2 982	3 109	4 663	3 195	5 230	4 292	2 928
Private short-term capital (net)	–4 034	–2 317	–1 185	–1 207	–588	–1 811	–690	–4 125	–3 255
Error and omission	–1 569	–162	–1 560	4 226	649	153	–1 113	91	–428
Overall balance (= change in foreign reserves)	–3 876	–464	–102	1 128	4 724	1 537	3 427	258	–755
Foreign reserves	21 040	19 800	19 698	20 826	25 550	27 087	30 514	30 772	30 007

Source: Compiled from Bank Negara Malaysia, *Monthly Statistical Bulletin*, Kuala Lumpur (various issues)

market rates of between 20 and 40 per cent in Singapore, which provided a hefty premium over a domestic rate of about 11 per cent, coupled with a weakening exchange rate for the ringgit.[10] Arbitrage between the two rates by money market dealers in both Singapore and Malaysia began putting pressure on the domestic interest rates in Malaysia. Thus policy makers became increasingly concerned about the 'internationalization' of the national currency, which carried a potential new threat to economic stability and monetary policy autonomy. The strong demand for offshore ringgits and the consequent build-up of offshore ringgit deposits increased the vulnerability of the ringgit, undermining the effectiveness of monetary policy (BNM, 1999b, ch. 14).

CONCLUDING REMARKS

The impressive growth trajectory of the Malaysian economy changed dramatically with the onset of the financial crisis. The currency and stock market turmoil that began in July 1997 was quickly translated into economic collapse. Unlike the other three crisis countries, Malaysia succumbed to the crisis with only a little foreign debt exposure of its banking system (discussed in Chapter 4). For this reason, Malaysian authorities were able to muddle through without an IMF-sponsored rescue package. Given the low reliance on offshore borrowing, the Malaysian corporations were not directly affected by massive currency depreciation. However, they had become highly vulnerable to domestic interest rate increases because of massive domestic debt build-up. Malaysia had by far the largest debt to GDP ratio among the crisis-hit countries (and in the world at large). In this context it was difficult to use the interest rate as a policy tool to support the exchange rate in the face of continuing capital outflow. By mid-1998, the economy was in deep recession and there were no signs of achieving currency and share price stability. In the absence of a clear policy anchor, indecisiveness had begun to hamper Malaysia's recovery process. Thus the stage was set for a dramatic policy turnaround.

NOTES

1. When all five countries are taken together, banks accounted for the bulk of the massive reversal of capital flows. Between 1996 and 1998, total net bank credit plummeted by almost $80 billion compared to a decline in inflows of portfolio equity by $10 billion (Williamson, 1999, p. 19).
2. Unless otherwise stated, data reported in this chapter come from Bank Negara Malaysia, *Monthly Statistical Bulletin* (various issues).
3. George Soros responded to Mahathir, saying that 'interfering with the convertibility of capital at a moment like this is a recipe for disaster' and that Dr Mahathir was 'a menace

to his own country'. For excerpts from statements made by Mahathir and Soros at the IMF meetings, see FPB (1997).

4. Until the onset of the crisis, Malaysia had 'the vast advantage over other Southeast Asian countries of political stability and policy continuity' (Radelet and Sachs, 1997, p. 56).
5. At a news conference following the inauguration of NEAC, Dr Mahathir resembled NEAC to the powerful National Operation Council formed in response to the May 1969 race riots.
6. For details on the structure, modalities and the underlying legal framework of these institutions, see BNM (1999b, pp. 220–25).
7. Ogus (2000, p. 45) observes a close resemblance between Malaysia's *Danaharta*/*Danamodel*/CDRC institutional framework and the Resolution Trust Corporation (RTC) in the USA, which was set up following the 1987 stock market crash to redress loan problems of the financial system.
8. The number of registered foreign workers declined by about 573 000 between 1997 and 1999. This figure needs to be interpreted with care because some of the previously registered workers would have chosen not to renew their permits and joined the ranks of illegal foreign workers (Kassim, 2000).
9. Singapore was formally separated from Malaysia in 1965 and the Kuala Lumpur Stock Exchange was split from the Stock Exchange of Singapore in 1970 (see Chapter 3). However, family ties and business connections continued to remain strong. Trade in shares of Malaysian companies in the informal CLOB market was a major activity of both Singaporean and Malaysian brokerage firms. Ringgit was the main, if not the sole, invoicing currency for thriving trade between the two countries (which accounted for over 30 per cent of Malaysia's total trade by the mid-1990s) and many Singaporean banks and individual money dealers were actively involved in ringgit trading. For details, see Tripathi *et al.* (1998). With these closer links with Singapore, Malaysian authorities were forced to impose restrictions on capital account transactions.
10. Why ringgit deposits fetched such high offshore rates (in Singapore) remains a puzzle. One possible explanation is that this was because of high demand for ringgits by hedge funds, which were trying to close out their short positions in that currency (EIU, 1998).

6. Policy turnaround: from muddling through to capital control

Economic collapse in the first half of 1998 propelled serious rethinking of policy directions by the Malaysian government. Choices available to the government had become severely limited, however. As we saw in the previous chapter, from about mid-1998, Malaysia had opted to embark on monetary and fiscal expansion to fight the recession, while letting the exchange rate fluctuate as it pleased in line with the vagaries of capital flows and changing market sentiment. In theory, the exchange rate should have gradually stabilized as the economy recovered from the slump on the back of expansionary macroeconomic policies coupled with corporate and banking restructuring, but, in the context of economic collapse triggered by a massive speculative attack on the currency, possible recovery through domestic policy itself is not enough to soothe shattered market sentiments if the market participants are suspicious of national action, particularly if the policies are inconsistent with those advocated by the IMF. This was an acute problem in Malaysia, given the nature of the initial unorthodox response and well-publicized concerns (real or hypothetical) at the time about government intervention to rescue politically connected corporations and banks. As Dr Mahathir put it, 'Trying to help companies and banks by restructuring and making credit available … is considered as bailouts and this will cause a loss of confidence on the part of market forces. The result will be further devaluation of the currency and fall in share prices' (Mahathir, 1998, p. 104).

A related hurdle was the difficulties involved in mobilizing resources. Reflecting, and adding to, shattered market confidence, international credit rating agencies were downgrading Malaysia's credit rating in rapid succession. Consequently, a planned attempt to issue sovereign bonds in the USA and Europe to raise US$2 billion for implementing the banking sector restructuring programme had to be shelved in late August 1998.

REJECTING THE IMF

In this volatile economic climate, the Malaysian government had to choose between two alternatives. The first was to obtain a 'good housekeeping seal' on its policies from the IMF. This would have stabilized the exchange rate, as in Korea and Thailand, setting the stage for applying Keynesian therapy to speed up the recovery. The second option was to resort to capital controls in order to combine fixed exchange rate with Keynesian policies, while ignoring vagaries of market sentiments.

As BNM correctly observed in its *1998 Annual Report* (p. 5), the root cause of the worsening economic situation was the market perception that Malaysia would be less committed to structural reforms since it was not under an IMF programme. By this time the IMF had significantly changed its original strategy of 'confidence building through macroeconomic contraction' in favour of expansionary macroeconomic policy. The four IMF programme countries in the region – Indonesia, Korea, Thailand and the Philippines – had already reformulated their policies along these lines with the blessing of the IMF. Thus, if Malaysia's reluctance to seek IMF support was based purely on differences of opinion relating to macroeconomic policy, that constraint had become less binding by this time.[1]

A widely expressed view in pro-government news commentaries in Malaysia is that Malaysia was not eligible for IMF support even if it wanted to seek such support because of its relatively strong balance of payments position and its relatively lower foreign debt (BNM, 1999a, p. 5; NEAC, 1999, p. 1). However, this view is not consistent with general IMF practice in assisting member countries in the event of an economic crisis and Malaysia's own economic conditions at the time. The Philippines, for example, received IMF assistance for managing the crisis, even though its balance of payments position was relatively sound and its external debt burden remained low (compared to Thailand and Korea). In 1998, following a speculative attack on its currency (the real) Brazil was able to obtain a back-up credit line from the IMF (primarily as a means of regaining market confidence), notwithstanding its sizable foreign exchange reserves (over $40 billion) (Krugman, 1999b, p. 111). Balance of payments need is only one of the eligibility criteria used by the IMF. In any case, Malaysia's foreign exchange reserves were not extraordinarily high at the time (about $15 billion, down from a pre-crisis level of $25 billion). Therefore, if desired, presumably Malaysia could have entered an IMF programme with back-up financial support for crisis management, including recapitalization of banks and corporate restructuring.

The real issue was that entering an IMF programme was not politically acceptable to the Malaysian leadership.[2] As we saw in Chapter 2, for nearly three decades NEP (subsequently renamed NDP) – perhaps the most comprehensive affirmative action policy package ever implemented in any country in the world – has been central to the Malaysian economic policy. Given the intimate links developed between business and government under this programme, naturally the positive stabilizing impact of any policy move had to be weighed against its potential negative effect on sociopolitical stability of the country (Crouch, 1998).[3] In his presidential address to the UMNO General Assembly on 19 June 1998, Prime Minister Mahathir summed up his position on this issue as follows:

> if we have to resort to the International Monetary Fund assistance …, the conditions imposed by the IMF will require us to open up our economy to foreigners. There will not be any *Bumiputra* quota as the New Economic Policy (NEP) is an injustice, and unacceptable to their liberal democracy (Mahathir, 1998, pp. 60–61).

Confronted with this policy dilemma, the Malaysian leadership opted for the second alternative, ending the policy uncertainty that had pervaded the policy scene for almost a year.[4] As noted, the lynchpin of new policy was insulating the domestic financial markets from short-term financial flows through capital controls. This was expected to set the stage for fixing the exchange rate and provide breathing space for vigorous pursuance of monetary and fiscal expansion to fight recession.

The rationale behind Malaysia's new policy shift can be explained in terms of the standard textbook exposition of the 'impossible trinity' (alternatively referred to as the 'three-cornered dilemma', or 'trilemma') of national policy making in a global economy. The national policy maker in a global economy with free capital mobility faces the problem of choosing from three policy scenarios: discretionary monetary policy, stable exchange rate and free capital mobility (allowing people to exchange money however they like). The policy dilemma here is that a country can have on a sustainable basis *at most* two of these three scenarios. The Malaysia policy turnaround involved giving up the third (maintaining free capital mobility) with a view to maintaining a fixed ('quasi-pegged') exchange rate while using monetary expansion to achieve internal balance. Of the remaining two policy combinations, retaining a fixed rate and free capital mobility while giving up monetary policy autonomy was simply a non-option for Malaysia at the time. That would result in a situation where money supply is determined independently of the central bank's policies by saving and portfolio decisions of the public. The third option – capital mobility coupled with monetary policy autonomy while compromising on exchange rate flexibility – is the one most favoured in the textbook wisdom. But, as we have already discussed, in Malaysia continued implementation of that option had become virtually impossible as the policy makers were not prepared to turn to the IMF to soothe shattered market sentiments. Of course, free capital mobility can be maintained while retaining *some* exchange rate fixity and monetary policy autonomy through sterilized intervention (Reisen, 1993). However, the success of such a policy requires, among other things, greater fiscal discipline which can be assured only under normal (non-crisis) economic circumstance.

While domestic considerations seem to have played the key role in this policy turnaround, by this time the use of capital control to gain breathing space for crisis management had also begun to receive a measure of legitimacy in the international economic policy debate (see Chapter 1). In particular, Krugman's (1998b) controversial piece in *Fortune* (appearing two weeks before the announcement of Malaysia's new policy package), which specifically argued for using capital controls as a crisis management tool, received wide publicity in Malaysia.[6] There was also growing attention paid to the newly emerging view that China and Taiwan, the two economies in the East Asian growth league with controls on short-term capital movements, fared much better than the rest of the region during the crisis. The recent experiences of countries like Chile and Slovenia in using capital controls to manage shorter-term capital inflows were also often cited in the media and government reports.[7]

The use of temporary capital control as a tool of stabilization policy is not new to Malaysian policy makers. As noted, during the period 1993–94, BNM successfully used capital *inflow* controls without experiencing adverse effect on Malaysia's long-term prospects for attracting foreign investment. In fact, as early as 30 July 1997 (two weeks after the speculative attack on the ringgit) Dr Mahathir hinted that the government was contemplating capital controls as a possible policy alternative (*Far Eastern Economic Review*, 1997a).

CAPITAL CONTROL-BASED POLICY PACKAGE

As a first step, on 31 August 1998, offshore trading of shares of Malaysian companies was banned with immediate effect in a move to freeze over-the-counter share trading in the central limit order book (CLOB) market in Singapore.[8] This was followed by the imposition of comprehensive controls over short-term capital flows (1 September) and fixing the exchange rate at RM3.80/$ (2 September).

As BNM clearly stated in its policy announcement, the fixing of the exchange rate was done while retaining the option of changing it when the underlying economic fundamentals changed. While the new fixed rate implied a mild appreciation of the ringgit from the average level for the previous three months (around RM4.18), it represented a 35 per cent depreciation against the pre-crisis levels of about RM2.5.

The new capital controls banned trading in ringgit instruments among offshore banks operating in Malaysia and stopped Malaysian financial institutions offering domestic credit facilities to non-resident banks and stockbrokers. With a view to stopping speculative trading in ringgits in overseas markets (predominantly in Singapore), the use of the ringgit as an invoicing currency in foreign trade was banned with immediate effect and legal tender on all ringgit deposits held outside the country was abolished with effect from 30 September. A 12-month withholding period was imposed on repatriation of proceeds (principal and profit) from foreign portfolio investment.[9] The other measures were restrictions on overseas investment by residents exceeding RM10 000 and a limit of RM1000 on Malaysian overseas travellers. A detailed listing of the new capital and exchange control measures is provided in Table A.2.

The controls were confined to short-term capital flows and aimed at making it harder for short-term portfolio investors to sell their shares and keep the proceeds, and for offshore hedge funds to drive down the currency (Table 6.1). With the exception of limits on foreign exchange for foreign travel by Malaysian citizens, there was no retreat from the country's long-standing commitment to an open trade and investment policy. No new direct controls were imposed on import and export trade. Profit remittances and repatriation

Table 6.1 Malaysia's selective capital and foreign exchange controls

Transactions subject to control	Transactions not subject to control
Ringgit-denominated transactions with non-residents	Current account transactions • trade transactions denominated in foreign currency
Outflow of short-term capital • one-year withholding period until 30 August 1998, • a three-tier tax (10%, 20%, 30%) on profit remittance between September 1998 and February 1999, • a 10% tax on profit remittance since February 1999	Repatriation of profits, interests, dividends, capital gains and rental income from FDI and similar forms of ringgit assets owned by non-residents
Import and export of ringgit (carriage on person)	
Export of foreign currency by citizens (carriage on person)	General payments by residents including those for education abroad
Outflow of Malaysian investment abroad	FDI inflows and outflows

Source: BNM (1999b, ch. 8).

of capital by foreign investors continued to remain free of control. Immediately following the imposition of capital controls, BNM did experiment with new regulatory procedures in this area, but these were swiftly removed in response to protests by these firms (Zefferys, 1999). Moreover, some new measures were introduced to further encourage FDI participation in the economy. These included allowing 100 per cent foreign ownership of new investment made before 31 December 2000 in domestic manufacturing, regardless of the degree of export orientation; increasing the foreign ownership share in the telecommunication project from 30 per cent to 69 per cent (under the condition that the ownership share is brought down to 49 per cent after five years) and in stockbroking companies and the insurance sector from a previous uniform level of 30 per cent to 49 per cent and 51 per cent, respectively; and relaxing restrictions on foreign investment in landed property to allow foreigners to purchase all types of properties above RM250 000 in new projects or projects which are less than 50 per cent completed (Abidin, 2000, p. 188).

Two notable changes were made in the capital control measures in 1999. First, in early February 1999, the original 12-month holding restriction on portfolio investment was replaced by a system of repatriation levy. Under this system, there were two sets of repatriation levy, depending on whether the funds entered the country before or after 15 February 1999. For investments made before 15 February, a three-tier levy was applied to the principal (the capital value) on how long the funds were retained in the country. For funds entered after 15 February, there was a two-tier levy on the repatriation of profits (but not on the principal): 30 per cent on profit made and repatriated within one year, and 10 per cent on profit repatriated after one year. In August 1999, the two-tier levy on profit repatriation was replaced by a unified 10 per cent levy. Under a further revision to capital controls announced on 27 October 2000, profit earned from foreign portfolio investments in the country for a period of more than one year was exempted from this levy. Second, an agreement between the KLSE and the Singapore Stock Exchange reached on 26 February 2000 provided for the transfer of the shares trapped in the CLOB market to the Malaysian stock exchange and allow trading to resume. Other than these changes, capital controls and the fixed exchange rate system have continued to provide the setting for recovery from the crisis through expansionary macroeconomic policy.

The replacement of the one-year moratorium on portfolio capital with an exit tax was widely interpreted in the financial press as a major backsliding from the original capital controls. However, in reality it was a pragmatic revision to *only one* element of the comprehensive controls. The motive behind this revision, which was introduced in consultation with key players in the capital market (Merrill Lynch, 1999), was to set the stage for managing capital inflows in the recovery phase. Together with the restrictions already in place on foreign short-term bank borrowing, the new tax on profit repatriation from portfolio investment was expected to discourage excessive reliance of Malaysian corporations on volatile foreign capital.

With the policy autonomy gained through the fixed exchange rate and capital controls, the government swiftly embarked on a recovery package consisting of two key elements: macroeconomic stimulants, and banking and corporate restructuring.

Reflationary Policy

The 1999 Budget presented (in October 1998) predicted an increase in the budget deficit from 1.8 per cent of GNP to 3.2 per cent in 1999. The 2000 Budget saw a further increase in the deficit to 4.4 per cent of GNP. On the expenditure side there were no major new proposals in either Budget beyond some moderate increase in funds earmarked for road and rail projects. The major sources of deficit expansion were tax cuts and new tax incentives. Among them, the key element was a total waiver of income tax in 1999[10] and an across-the-board one percentage point reduction in income tax rates proposed for 2000. There were also tax breaks for industries of 'national and strategic importance' and import duty reduction on machinery and equipment imports. Benefiting from the new capital outflow controls, the government has been able to finance the deficits through issuing Malaysian government securities (MGS) that will be absorbed largely by provident, pension and insurance funds. Only about a third of the financial needs have been raised externally, mainly from concessionary bilateral and multilateral sources.

The increase in government expenditure was financed mainly domestically (86 per cent) with external borrowing contributing the remainder. Domestic borrowing came from the centrally controlled Employees Provident Fund and other saving funds, along with the cash-rich national oil monopoly, Petronas. In mobilizing external resources, the government relied primarily on concessionary long-term credit from multilateral sources (such as the World Bank, the Asian Development Bank (ADB) and the Islamic Development Bank) and bilateral borrowing from Japan under the new Miyasawa Initiative, Japanese Overseas Cooperation Fund and Japan Import–Export Bank. An exception was the US$1 billion global bond issue made in May 1999. The motive behind this was primarily to test the market following the imposition of capital controls. Throughout the crisis period, Malaysia remained a net creditor to the International Monetary Fund.[11]

To complement expansionary budgetary policy, BNM set out on a course of monetary expansion. The statutory reserve requirement (SRR) ratio for banking institutions was cut in successive stages in order to inject liquidity into the debt-ridden banking system. By late 1998, the ratio had come down to 4 per cent, against a pre-crisis level of 13.5 per cent. BNM also revised the formula used in computing the base lending rate (BLR)[12] so that reductions in the intervention rate are better reflected in cost of bank credit. The margin that banks could charge their customers above the BLR was reduced from 4 per cent to 2.5 per cent. The three-month inter-bank rate (BNM's policy rate on which other short-term interest rates are based), which was raised from 10 per cent to 11 per cent in February 1998 to defend the exchange rate, was reduced by a number of stages to 4 per cent by early 1999. The default period for reclassification of bank loans (which was reduced to three months from six months in January 1998) was changed back to six months, with a view to reducing the pressure on the bank to set aside capital against non-performing loans. The other measures introduced to boost credit expansion included an announcement on 9 September of an indicative annual loan growth target of 8 per cent for commercial banks, relaxation of credit limits on lending by commercial banks and financial companies for purchase of property and shares, a scheme for providing soft loans for purchase of cars, a special loan scheme for assisting smaller industries and low-income groups, and relaxing credit limits on credit cards (BNM, 1999a).

When taken as a whole, a noteworthy feature of the Malaysian macroeconomic stimulant package so far has been the relatively high weight assigned to monetary policy compared to fiscal policy. One consideration behind this policy choice was the need to avoid crowding out on the private sector investment expansion/recovery, which had been adversely affected by interest rate hikes and the credit squeeze. Another, and perhaps the more important, consideration was institutional bottlenecks impinging on speedy implementation of new government projects.[13] Whatever the underlying reason may be, the greater emphasis placed on monetary policy than on fiscal policy was presumably a major factor in the choice of capital controls as a pivotal element of the reform package. To use monetary policy for internal balance, in violation of the 'Mundell assignment' of using fiscal policy for internal balance and monetary policy for external balance (Mundell, 1968), essentially requires capital controls to insulate the economy against international capital movement (Branson, 1993, p. 34).

Banking and Corporate Restructuring

The new policy package placed greater emphasis on the speedy implementation of the banking and corporate restructuring programmes initiated in the first half of 1998. To recapitulate, the programme involved carving out bad debt from the banking system by *Danaharta* (the National Asset Management Company), injection of fresh capital through *Danamodal* (Bank

Recapitalization Company) and The Corporate Debt Restructuring Committee (CDRC). This well-thought-out programme remained virtually inactive, because of difficulties involved in raising the required funds. The new policy framework provided a conducive setting for raising required funds from domestic sources.

In addition to these bad debt carving out and recapitalization schemes, BNM embarked on ambitious merger programmes for domestic finance companies and banks, with a view to improving their competitiveness. The merger programme for finance companies, which aimed at reducing the number of finance companies from 39 to less than half that number through merger and/or amalgamation with banks, has already been completed. The banking merger programme aimed to consolidate the nation's 58 financial institutions into six (subsequently increased to ten) banking groups.

CONCLUDING REMARKS

The Malaysian decision at the beginning of September 1998 to cut loose from the IMF orthodoxy was an important policy experiment arising from the East Asian crisis. The decision involved the imposition of comprehensive capital outflow controls in order to regain macroeconomic policy autonomy and exchange rate stability. This policy choice was expected to provide the Malaysian authorities with breathing space to engineer the recovery through monetary expansion and fiscal pump priming, while affecting needed banking and corporate sector reforms without being subject to vagaries of market sentiment. Apart from the replacement of the moratorium originally imposed on outflow of foreign portfolio capital by a duty on foreign remittances, the new comprehensive capital control package continued to provide cover for crisis management.

Political scientists will continue to debate the relative importance of pure political motives compared to genuine economic policy considerations behind this policy shift. But the fact remains that Malaysia's social equilibrium is more fragile than that of the socially homogeneous countries like Thailand and Korea. There is little doubt among informed Malaysia observers that the affirmative action policy enshrined in NEP had played a crucial role in the country's impressive economic success, as against generally dismal economic records of other heterogeneous, multi-ethnic nations in the developing world. In this context, there was a strong case for the Malaysian policy makers to act on their own judgment of which approach to crisis management was in their best interest. The real issue is whether the radical policy choice was instrumental in ushering in recovery.

NOTES

1. In a public lecture given in Kuala Lumpur a month after the imposition of capital controls, Bhagwati (1998b) argued on these grounds that the 'Malaysia option should have been to stay the course and work with the IMF'.
2. It is pertinent to note here that Malaysia managed its mid-1980s crisis on its own, while eschewing IMF support. As in the context of the 1997–8 crisis, political imperatives on which the NEP is based were the prime consideration behind this policy choice (Narayanan, 1996).
3. The political commentators will continue to debate the relative importance of the pure political objective of bailing out politically related companies and the genuine social stability concerns in explaining Malaysia's reluctance to accept IMF support. Some commentators argue that, given profound socioeconomic changes over past two decades, a spontaneous outbreak of racial violence is now highly unlikely in Malaysia (Hiebert and Jayasankaran, 1999). However, the fact remains that Malaysian social equilibrium is more fragile than that of the socially homogeneous countries such as Thailand and Korea (Crouch, 1996, 1998; Stiglitz, 2000). Race relations did deteriorate in the mid-1980s following a modest economic downturn (1 per cent contraction of GDP).
4. To set the stage for the policy turnaround, Anwar (who had been pushing reforms along IMF lines) was sidelined from the policy scene by the appointment of Daim Zainuddin (Mahathir's long-time policy adviser) as the minister of special functions, a portfolio newly created for handling crisis management. On 2 September, Anwar was removed from the positions of deputy prime minister and finance minister. He was subsequently expelled from the United Malay National Organisation (the major party in the ruling coalition). On 7 September, Mahathir appointed himself the first finance minister. This position was subsequently assigned to Zainuddin, in addition to his role as the minister of special functions. One interpretation of the almost simultaneous occurrence of the sacking of Anwar and the announcement of a new reform package is that the prime motive of the latter was to set the stage for sacking Anwar without a visible display of market disappointment and precipitation of currency and share market collapse.
5. For a non-technical, yet lucid, exposition of the impossible trinity, see Krugman (1999b, pp. 106–7).
6. However, it is not correct to name (as some authors, such as Miller, 1999 and Hale, 1998, have done) Krugman as the intellectual architect of the Malaysia policy turnaround. Apparently, the decision to introduce capital control was made by the National Economic Action Council on 6 August (Mahathir, 1999b), before the Krugman article appeared. Krugman subsequently stated in Singapore, 'It was a shock that while I was speculating idly about that [capital control], Dr. Mahathir was about to do it' (*New Straits Times*, 26 August 1999). See also Krugman (1999b).
7. In a special briefing to the press following the introduction of capital controls, the special function minister, Zainuddin, stated that before introducing currency controls the Malaysian authorities studied systems operating in Chile, Slovenia and China, and decided to use the Chinese system as a model in designing the Malaysian controls (*Star*, 5 September 1998).
8. The CLOB market was an informal market for shares of Malaysian companies, which operated side-by-side with the formal share market (Singapore Stock Exchange) in Singapore. At the time, total value of Malaysian shares traded in CLOB amounted to US$4.2 billion (*Far Eastern Economic Review*, 9 March 1999, p. 56). Short selling of shares continued on this market after such share dealings were made illegal in Malaysia following the onset of the crisis, and this was perceived by policy makers in Malaysia as a major factor behind exchange rate and share price instability. CLOB trading was also thought to contribute to ringgit outflow to Singapore. Following the Malaysian move to ban offshore trading of Malaysian company shares, the CLOB market was closed on 15 September.
9. This restriction reportedly blocked $10 billion of foreign investment in domestic securities.

10. The waiver was part of a change in Malaysia's tax assessment system, beginning in the year 2000, from one based on income derived in the previous year to income derived in the current year.
11. Malaysia's lending to the IMF was in the form of ringgit loans for use by IMF programme countries. Malaysia was not eligible to make use of IMF finance under normal credit tranche facilities because there was no balance of payments need.
12. The benchmark interest rate prescribed by BNM for a lending institution with a view to avoiding unhealthy competition in credit markets.
13. For instance, the 1999 Budget predicted a deficit of 6.1 per cent of GNP, but as noted the outcome was eventually a deficit of only 3.2 per cent of GNP.

7. The recovery

After identifying the nature and underlying rationale of Malaysia's capital control-based reform package, we come now to the central question of our study: has this policy turnaround been successful in ushering in recovery? This chapter sets the stage for answering this question by presenting an account of the recovery process. The next chapter will attempt to delineate the role of capital control in the recovery process.

OVERALL PATTERNS

The Malaysian economy experienced a 7.5 per cent contraction in GDP in 1998, after 11 years of uninterrupted expansion averaging 8.0 per cent per year. This was by far the worst downturn since the Second World War; GDP contracted by a mere 1.0 per cent during the mid-1980s crisis. The degree of output contraction moderated to 1.3 per cent (on an annual basis) in the first quarter of 1999, followed by a positive growth rate of 4.1 per cent in the second quarter (Table 7.1, Figure 7.1). Recovery accelerated in the next two quarters, culminating in a growth rate of 5.4 per cent for the whole year. An 11.7 per cent growth rate was recorded in the first quarter of 2000, followed by 8.8 per cent in the second quarter. Growth in the first half of 2000 was 4.7 per cent, compared to 1.8 per cent for the same period in the previous year. Thus the economy had regained the pre-crisis (1996) level of GDP by mid-2000, leaving behind almost two 'lost' years. At the time of writing this book (September 2000) the official annual growth forecast for 2000 remained at 5.8 per cent (after two rounds of upward revision from 4 per cent), but various independent analysts were predicting higher growth rates, in the range of 6–8 per cent.

In line with strong recovery in domestic production, the employment situation has improved. According to the Survey of Retrenchments (conducted by the Department of Labour), the number of workers stood off declined from the post-crisis peak of 18 116 in the fourth quarter of 1998 to 7909 in the fourth quarter of 1999. The end-of-year number of job seekers registered with the Manpower Department declined from 54 318 in 1998 to 31 830 in 1999. The unemployment rate in the economy by the end of 1999 stood at 3.4 per cent, only 0.9 percentage points higher than the pre-crisis level.

Table 7.1 Malaysia: selected economic indicators, 1997Q1–2000Q2[1]

	1996	1997	1998	1999	97Q1	97Q2	97Q3	97Q4	98Q1	98Q2	98Q3	98Q4	99Q1	99Q2	99Q3	99Q4	00Q1	00Q2
Growth of GDP (%)	10.0	7.3	–7.4	5.6	7.6	8.4	7.2	6.1	–1.6	–5.9	–10.1	–11.2	–1.5	4.8	8.5	10.8	11.7	—
Growth by final demand category[2] (%)																		
Consumption (59.3)	4.9	4.9	–10.3	6.7	5.5	8.3	2.9	4.6	–8.1	–6.0	–10.7	–148	0.5	2.9	8.3	9.9	12.1	—
Private (45.6)	6.9	4.3	–10.8	3.1	2.6	6.7	6.4	2.0	–5.4	–8.9	–14.9	–13.8	–2.1	–2.8	4.6	7.0	14.4	—
Public (13.7)	0.7	7.6	–7.8	16.3	14.6	15.2	–8.1	12.7	–16.8	3.1	2.3	–17.9	15.7	20.8	20.2	19.6	1.0	—
Gross domestic fixed investment (46.8)	9.7	8.4	–44.9	–5.9	6.1	32.4	13.6	15.0	–17.3	–49.0	–50.8	–50.5	–29.6	–12.6	5.1	6.0	12.3	—
Private (34.2)	13.3	8.4	–57.8	–18.5	—	—	—	—	—	—	—	—	—	—	—	—	—	—
Public (12.6)	1.1	8.6	–10.0	11.7	—	—	—	—	—	—	—	—	—	—	—	—	—	—
Growth by sector (%)[2]																		
Agriculture, forestry and fishing (9.8)	4.5	0.4	–4.5	3.9	1.8	3.9	–1.5	–2.1	–2	–6.9	–4	–4.7	–4.1	8.4	2.9	4.5	2.9	—
Industry (41.5)	11.0	10.5	–6.5	5.4	10.2	8.4	9.1	8.8	–5.6	–9.4	–16.2	–15.4	–3.1	5.7	—	—	—	—
Mining and quarrying (7.7)	2.9	1.9	–0.8	1.3	–1.7	1.2	0.8	7.5	0.9	0.7	1.8	0.1	–2.9	–4.6	–0.1	–4.8	0.8	—
Manufacturing (29.1)	18.2	10.1	–13.4	13.5	11.3	9.1	10.8	9.4	–5.0	–9.6	–18.6	–19.3	–0.2	10.7	19.8	24.2	27.3	—
Construction (4.7)	16.2	10.6	–23.0	–5.6	17.5	10.8	7.3	7.8	–14.5	–19.8	–28.0	–29.0	–16.6	–7.9	0.9	2.7	1.2	—
Services (48.7)	8.9	9.9	–0.7	3.1	10.2	12.4	10.5	6.8	4.7	0.0	–3.1	–3.9	0.1	1.5	4.2	6.0	6.3	—
Growth of manufacturing production[3] (%)	11.1	10.6	–7.2	8.9	13.3	11.6	9.6	10.1	–2.9	–8.9	–13.4	–15.4	–0.3	15.7	20.0	24.7	32.1	24.8
Export-oriented (weight: 0.52)	8.8	13.1	–7.7	12.8	13.3	12.7	9.6	10.8	0.1	–5.3	–11.3	–12.2	–1.0	16.7	17.5	24.5	38.2	29.3
Domestic-oriented (weight: 0.48)	16.2	14.6	–13.4	13.1	13.3	10.4	9.7	9.3	–6.1	–12.8	–15.6	–18.3	0.4	14.6	22.0	25.0	25.2	20.6
Imports of investment goods (growth of value, %)	–6.4	17.0	–15.3	–8.9	—	—	—	—	30.4	–32.2	–15.6	–31.1	–39.0	–12.2	5.3	21.6	37.1	63.1
MIER consumer sentiments index (1988 = 100)	128.4	121.9	82.0	103.7	127.2	133.4	122.1	104.9	88.5	79.1	80.0	80.5	84.0	101.6	111.3	117.7	123.5	—
MIER business conditions index	58.0	59.2	42.5	57.9	62.9	65.2	57.5	49.6	41.0	42.3	41.8	44.7	48.5	60.3	62.2	61.0	71.3	—

Table 7.1 continued

	1996	1997	1998	1999	97Q1	97Q2	97Q3	97Q4	98Q1	98Q2	98Q3	98Q4	99Q1	99Q2	99Q3	99Q4	00Q1	00Q2
MIER manufacturing capacity utilization index	81.2	83.2	59.5	80.7	87.4	86.1	87.4	85.4	80.6	76.4	76.6	76.4	77.9	92.4	92.4	92.2	93.1	—
Unemployment rate	2.5	2.6	3.2	3.4	3.1	2.9	2.8	3.1	3.3	3.2	3.3	3.4	4.5	3.3	2.9	3.0	—	—
Inflation rate (%)																		
Consumer price	3.5	2.7	5.3	2.8	3.2	2.5	2.3	2.7	4.3	5.7	5.6	5.4	4.0	2.7	2.3	2.1	1.5	1.5
Producer price	2.3	2.7	10.7	–3.5	2.7	–0.5	1.0	7.2	11.9	13.9	13.9	3.9	–4.1	–5.0	–4.3	–0.3	3.9	5.6
Domestic goods	2.8	2.5	11.2	–3.9	3.0	–0.9	0.6	7.5	12.0	14.5	15.0	3.8	–4.0	–5.9	–5.0	0.7	4.6	6.7
Imported goods	0.1	2.8	9.2	–0.6	1.4	1.0	2.7	5.9	11.3	11.3	9.6	4.8	–0.3	–0.8	–1.0	–0.1	1.1	1.1
Fiscal performance (central government)																		
Government expenditure as % of GDP	23.0	23.3	19.9	19.6	22.0	23.6	23.0	24.5	19.5	19.9	20.0	20.4	19.3	20.3	18.9	19.9	14.2	—
Gross development expenditure as % of total expenditure	25.1	24.0	31.9	38.5	10.8	20.3	18.6	34.8	8.5	17.1	24.8	69.1	6.6	35.4	51.4	48.9	21.5	—
Budget deficit (central government) as % of GDP	0.7	2.4	–1.8	–3.2	1.5	1.4	1.0	–1.3	1.5	–0.1	0.5	–3.6	1.1	–0.1	–1.7	–2.4	0.3	—
Total public debt as % of GDP	35.3	31.9	36.2	35.9	32.9	31.4	31.6	31.9	30.5	31.2	30.7	36.2	36.9	38.5	37.7	35.9	35.5	—
Foreign as % of total public debt (%)	11.7	14.4	14.5	16.6	11.5	10.8	12.7	14.4	12.7	14.7	13.6	14.5	13.3	16.1	16.1	16.6	16.1	—
Money and credit (end of period)																		
M3 growth (%)	21.2	18.5	2.8	8.2	24.7	21.1	22.6	18.5	12.1	8.7	7.6	2.8	3.9	7.7	8.2	8.2	5.8	4.1
Average bank lending rate (%)	10.1	10.6	12.3	8.5	10.1	10.5	10.7	11.2	12.5	13.5	12.6	10.0	9.6	8.7	8.1	7.8	7.8	7.7
Outstanding loans of banking system (Ringgit billion)[4]	325	586	482	672	—	—	—	586	510	541	587	642	607	620	628	672	685	633
Loans extended by the banking system (growth, %)	26.7	26.5	1.3	0.6	—	—	—	26.5	16.9	10.2	4.5	1.3	1.3	2.5	2.4	0.8	1.4	2.1
Manufacturing	14.8	18.5	2.0	1.3	—	—	—	18.5	10.5	12.3	10.2	2.9	–2.9	1.5	2.6	1.3	3.5	2.2
Property	26.8	34.0	6.9	–6.6	—	—	—	34.0	27.9	20.1	11.6	6.9	5.7	–5.8	–5.3	–6.6	–7.2	8.0

Non-performing loans as % of total loans[5,6]	7.8	5.5	3.7	4.1	—	—	—	5.5	7.0	8.9	8.1	8.6	7.9	7.9	7.7	6.6	6.5	6.2
Share market performance																		
KLSE Composite index	1238	594	586	812	1203	1077	815	594	720	456	374	586	503	870	736	763	922	881
Market capitalization (ringgit billions)	807	376	375	553	845	745	585	376	453	286	249	375	318	503	490	561	632	616
External transactions																		
Merchandise exports (US$, FOB, %)	6.0	0.3	–6.9	15.7	7.6	0.4	2.7	–4.3	–10.7	–8.7	–10.9	6.5	5.5	15.3	21.5	19.2	21.9	—
Merchandise imports (US$, FOB, %)	1.0	0.2	–25.9	12.5	2.3	1.3	1.8	–7.6	–20.3	–33.9	–29.3	–20.2	–6.1	10.0	21.4	25.6	27.1	—
Current account balance as % of GDP	–4.8	–5.3	13.0	15.9	–3.8	–11.3	–3.0	–2.5	6.4	11.3	17.9	16.5	16.5	19.1	17.9	13.4	—	—
Foreign reserves (US$ billion)[5]	27.0	20.8	25.6	30.9	27.7	26.6	22.1	20.7	19.8	19.7	20.7	25.6	27.1	30.6	31.1	30.9	33.9	33.5
Total external debt as % GDP[3]	38.7	43.9	42.6	42.1	—	—	—	43.9	47.9	51.2	53.0	58.8	57.8	57.7	56.9	53.3	51.5	51.3
Short-term foreign debt as % of total debt[5]	25.7	25.2	19.9	14.3	—	—	—	—	25.1	22.8	19.1	19.9	19.7	18.5	17.1	14.3	13.3	12.5
Short-term foreign debt as % of foreign reserves[5]	36.9	53.7	33.2	—	—	—	—	—	54.6	48.9	37.0	33.2	30.6	25.8	23.9	23.6	16.1	15.0
External debt service ratio	6.6	5.5	6.7	5.9	7.5	5.4	4.3	5.1	7.2	7.1	6.4	6.1	6.9	4.4	5.3	7.0	4.2	—
Average exchange rate (ringgit per US$)	2.5	2.8	3.9	3.8	2.5	2.5	2.8	3.5	4.0	3.8	4.1	3.8	3.8	3.8	3.8	3.8	3.8	3.8

Notes:
1. All growth rates on a year-on-year basis.
2. Sectoral share in GDP in 1996 is given in brackets.
3. Based on manufacturing production index (1993 = 100). The weight attached to each category in the total index is given in brackets.
4 Net of non-performing loans (six-month definition).
5. End of period.
6. Non-performing loans of commercial banks only. Based on a 'six month' non-performing period.

— data not available.
FOB Free on board.
MIER Malaysian Institute of Economic Research.

Source: Compiled from Bank Negara Malaysia, *Monthly Statistical Bulletin* (updated for the latest quarters using data from the Bank's web site: *www.bnm.gov.my*) and MIER, *Monthly Economic Monitor* (various issues).

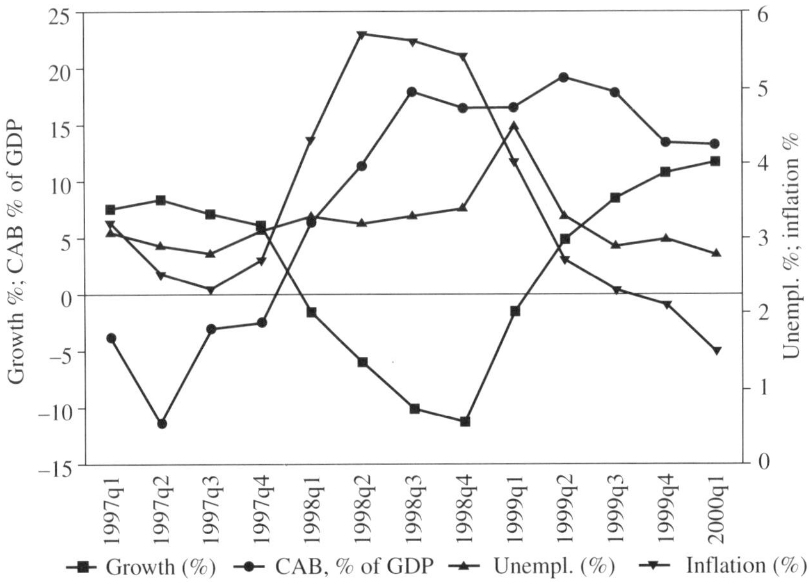

Source: Table 7.1.

Figure 7.1 GDP growth, current account balance, unemployment and inflation in Malaysia, 1997Q1–2000Q1

The recovery process was underpinned by remarkably low inflation, despite the heavy emphasis on fiscal and monetary expansion as part of the recovery strategy. The annual rate of consumer price inflation increased from 2.7 per cent to 5.3 per cent between 1997 and 1998. The rate of inflation measured in terms of the producer price index increased from 2.7 per cent to 10.7 per cent between 1997 and 1998 and then declined to 3.2 per cent in 1999. The relative higher inflation measured in terms of the producer price index for 1998 and 1999 seems to reflect the price-raising impact of massive currency depreciation.

Growing business confidence in the recovery process began to be reflected in an impressive recovery in trading on the Kuala Lumpur Stock Exchange (KLSE) from mid-1999. The benchmark Kuala Lumpur Composite Index (KLCI) had almost regained its pre-crisis (end of June 1997) level by end of February 2000. Market capitalization of the KLSE increased from the historical low of RM200 billion in August 1998 to over RM700 billion in February 2000, which was only five percentage points short of the pre-crisis (June 1997) level. The consumer sentiment and business confidence indices of MIER were also rapidly approaching the pre-crisis levels.

DOMESTIC DEMAND

Reflecting the impact of reflationary policy, public expenditure led the way to recovery. Following a 7.8 per cent contraction in 1998, public consumption recorded double-digit growth from the first quarter of 1999, contributing to over 70 per cent of the total consumption growth of 6.7 per cent in that year. Public fixed investment contracted by only 10 per cent in 1998, compared to a 58 per cent contraction in private fixed investment. In 1999, the public fixed investment expanded by 14 per cent in a context of continued contraction in private investment (though at a lower rate), slowing contraction in total annual investment to 6 per cent, compared to a 45 per cent contraction in the previous year.

Private consumption was seen to be stabilizing in the first half of 1999 and grew strongly in the second half of the year. In the first quarter of 2000, private consumption grew by 14 per cent, yielding a 12 per cent expansion in total consumption despite a slowing down of public consumption to a mere 1 per cent (compared to over 10 per cent growth in the four previous quarters).

Private investment continued to contract in 1999, though at a much slower rate (12 per cent), compared to a massive contraction (57 per cent) in the previous year. While quarterly private investment estimates are not available, according to available leading indicators of investment behaviour, private investment would have started recovering from about the final quarter of 1999. For instance, imports of machinery, which contracted for five consecutive quarters from 1988Q1, started recovering from 1999Q3, and the first two quarters of 2000 recorded growth rates of 37 per cent and 63 per cent, respectively. Two other leading indicators reported in the table – MIER's business sentiment index and growth of loans extended by the banking system (to the manufacturing sector in particular) – also corroborate this pattern. The delayed recovery of private investment is consistent with the existing excess capacity and stock overhang in the economy.[1]

SECTORAL PATTERNS

On the production side, signs of recovery emerged first in the services sectors (particularly in financial services) and domestic market-oriented manufacturing. By the second quarter of 1999, recovery had become more broad-based, with export-oriented manufacturing playing a leading role. During 1999Q2–2000Q2, growth of export-oriented manufacturing was almost twice as fast as domestic-oriented manufacturing (see Figure 7.2). Of the total increment of manufacturing production during this period, 68 per cent originated in export-oriented manufacturing. Of the total increment in GDP during this

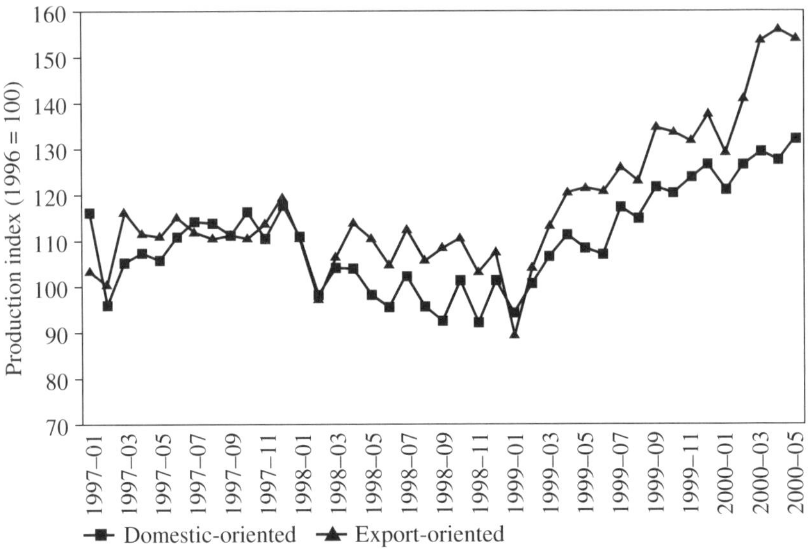

Source: Bank Negara Malaysia, *Monthly Statistical Bulletin*, Kuala Lumpur (various issues).

Figure 7.2 Indices of export-oriented and domestic-oriented manufacturing output in Malaysia (1996= 100), January 1997–May 2000

period, over 70 per cent came from the manufacturing sector, with almost 47 per cent coming from export-oriented manufacturing alone. Thus the Malaysian experience through the crisis is consistent with the conventional wisdom that greater export orientation is an important facilitator of economic rebound following a crisis (Bhagwati, 1998b; Sachs, 1985).

The main source of manufacturing growth in the second half of 1999 was the MNE-dominated electronics sub-sector, while other export-oriented industries such as processed foods, plastic and rubber goods, and domestic market-oriented industries, also continued to record impressive growth, benefiting from significant improvement in international competitiveness brought about by exchange rate depreciation. Within the global electronics industry, the semiconductor cycle recorded an upturn in 1998, aided by the Year 2000 phenomenon, after an unprecedented three-year lull from mid-1996. Rebound in this product sector was of considerable significance for Malaysia as electronics accounted for over 20 per cent of manufacturing output and 50 per cent of total exports at the onset of the crisis. By late 1999, electronics firms in Malaysia were operating at full capacity, while the production capacity had been expanding rapidly, with many electronics MNEs relocating their production bases to Malaysia from Singapore (World Bank, 2000). Apart from the upturn in the world electronics cycle, the lower cost structure and the competitive exchange rate in Malaysia, strong recovery of external demand following improvement in economic conditions in East Asia and continued robust growth in the USA were instrumental in the expansion of output in the export-oriented manufacturing sector.

The agricultural sector (including forestry and fishing) recorded negative growth in 1997 and 1998, reflecting world market conditions for the major primary export products, (in particular rubber and palm oil), adding to the crisis-driven collapse of growth. This sector began to record positive growth from the second quarter of 1999, underpinned by a sharp rebound in palm oil output, from a decline of 8.3 per cent in 1998 to an estimated increase of 19.4 per cent in 1999. The mining sector, however, recorded a marginal decline of 1.2 per cent in 1999, reflecting a decline in domestic demand for gas in the depressed economy and some curtailment of crude oil production under the government's National Depletion Policy.

The services sector grew by 6 per cent in 1999, with all sub-sectors showing strong growth, reflecting across-the-board improvements in final demand, in particular robust trade performance and strong recovery in consumer demand. The construction sector was the hardest hit by the crisis. In 1998, value added in this sector contracted by a staggering 23.5 per cent, accounting for over one-third of total GDP contraction (of 7.5 per cent) in the year. Reflecting the severity of asset market collapse, the process of contraction continued well into the third quarter of 1999.

FISCAL POSITION

As discussed in Chapter 5, by mid-1998 the Malaysian government reversed the contractionary fiscal policies introduced following the onset of the crisis. Reflecting the new expansionary measures, the central government Budget recorded a deficit amounting to 1.8 per cent of GDP in 1998 for the first time since 1992. The budget deficit increased further, to 3.8 per cent of GDP, in 1999 as a result of the intensification of expansionary policies as part of the September 1998 policy package. Given strong revenue growth in a rapidly recovering economy, many analysts predict the budget deficit in 2000 to be much smaller than was predicted (4.4 per cent of GDP) in the 2000 Budget speech. Quarterly data in fact point to a slight decline in the deficit from about the third quarter of 1999 (after making allowance for regular quarterly oscillations).

While the initial impetus for recovery came from fiscal pump priming, over time the recovery has become increasingly private sector-led, with private consumption and net exports providing much of the stimulant for output growth. Therefore the government was in a position to consolidate the fiscal position with the aim of achieving a surplus budget perhaps within the next two years.

Interestingly, government expenditure relative to GDP declined from the pre-crisis (1996) level of 23 per cent to 20 per cent in 1999. At the same time, the share of gross development expenditure in total expenditure increased from 25 per cent to 39 per cent between these two years. These figures taken together suggest that, despite the commitment to fiscal expansion as part of the recovery strategy, the government has taken due care to keep current expenditure under control. Current expenditure, as a percentage of total government revenue, remained virtually unchanged, at the pre-crisis level of 56 per cent.

Financing of the 1998 budget deficit involved an increase of net total borrowing by RM12.8 billion. This was the first increase in net public borrowing after six consecutive years of debt redemption. In 1999, net total borrowing increased by another RM8.3 billion. Consequently, the end-of-year public debt stock as a share of GDP increased from 32 per cent in 1996 to 36 per cent in 1998 and remained at the same level in 1999. Almost 85 per cent of the addition to total debt stock in 1998 and 1999 came from domestic borrowing. However, the share of foreign debt in the total stock did increase from 12 per cent to 16.6 per cent between 1996 and 1999. But much of foreign borrowing (over 80 per cent) was long-term concessionary loans obtained from multilateral financial organizations and foreign governments. In sum, Malaysia has been able to ride out the crisis without building up a massive debt overhang.[2]

EXTERNAL POSITION

The turnaround in real GDP growth has been accompanied by a further strengthening of the balance of payments position, driven by a more favourable external trade balance and significant inflows of long-term capital (Table 7.1).

Boosted by strong export performance, which outpaced import growth, the trade balance recorded a surplus of RM74 billion in 1999, 7.4 per cent higher than the surplus registered in 1998. After allowing for a larger deficit in the services account (due to a larger net payment of investment income as a result of the higher level of profits and dividends), the current account recorded an unprecedented surplus of 15 per cent of GDP, up from 13.7 per cent of GDP in the previous year. The surplus on the long-term capital account of the balance of payments increased marginally, from 1 per cent in

1998 to 1.3 per cent in 1999. This increase reflected an increase in foreign borrowing by the federal government and non-profit public enterprises. Net FDI inflows remained virtually unchanged at the level of the previous year.

By the end of 1999, Malaysia's foreign exchange reserves stood at US$31 billion, and they provided 300 per cent cover for total outstanding short-term debts and 200 per cent cover for the stock of volatile capital (outstanding short-term debt plus cumulating portfolio investment, as defined in Chapter 4) of the country. Total external debt as a percentage of GDP increased from 44 per cent in 1997 to 58 per cent in 1998, and then declined to 53 per cent in 1999. The share of short-term debt in total outstanding debt declined from 25.2 per cent in 1977 to 19.9 per cent in 1998 and then to 14.3 per cent in 1999.

CONCLUDING REMARKS

The Malaysian economy began to recover from its worst recession in the post-independence era from about the third quarter of 1999. By mid-2000, the economy was back to the pre-crisis output level, although with almost two years 'lost' from the projected growth trajectory towards achieving developed country status. Although export-oriented industries have played an important role, the recovery is not entirely export-led. Domestic demand expansion triggered by an expansionary macroeconomic policy has played a pivotal role in achieving a broad-based recovery.

With emerging signs of recovery, critics began to acknowledge by late 1999 that the radical reform measures worked well in Malaysia (or, in any case, are doing no demonstrable harm) contrary to their initial scepticism. Major international credit-rating agencies, which downgraded Malaysia's rating immediately following the imposition of capital control, came up with more optimistic assessments of prospects. The IMF, in its latest Public Information Notices on the recent *Article IV Consultation with Malaysia*, commended the Malaysian authorities for 'using the breathing space [provided by the policy measures introduced in September 1998] to push ahead with a well-designed and effectively implemented strategy for financial sector restructuring' (IMF, 1999a, 2000). The Washington-based private think-tank, the Economic Strategic Institute, noted in late 1999 that, 'despite the bad press it gets as a result of Prime Minister Mahathir's critical comments about speculators, Malaysia is the best story in the region' (Economic Strategy Institute, 1999).

NOTES

1. According to the Survey of Business Sentiments of MIER, capacity utilization in domestic manufacturing in the first quarter of 1999 was 75 per cent, compared with the annual average of 85 per cent for 1987–96. While there was no satisfactory indicator, excess capacity in the building and construction sector was presumably much greater.
2. This point will be discussed in the next chapter as part of the analysis of the impact of capital control on crisis management.

8. The role of capital controls

In the previous chapter we saw that the Malaysian economy began to show strong signs of recovery following the introduction of the capital control-based reform package. But how far has the radical policy shift actually contributed to the turnaround?

Many observers have attempted to answer this question through simple comparisons of recovery experiences of crisis-hit countries using readily available performance indicators. A common inference from such comparisons is that controls have not made a 'distinct' contribution to the recovery process in Malaysia – not only Malaysia but also the other crisis-hit Asian countries, which maintained open capital accounts throughout under IMF-centred reform packages, began to recover about the same time (Hiebert, 1999; IMF, 1999b; Miller, 1999; Lim, 1999). This view is not quite consistent with the available performance indicators, however. While all crisis-hit countries started to show signs of recovery from about late 1998, only Korea has so far recorded a faster recovery rate than Malaysia. But Korea is a mature industrial nation with a diversified manufacturing base. Moreover, the dominant role played by a few national companies (*chaebols*) in manufacturing production and trade seems to have placed Korea in a uniquely advantageous position in the recovery process (Booth, 1999). In terms of the stage of development and the nature of the economic structures, undoubtedly the better comparator for Malaysia is Thailand.

Malaysia's recovery rate has so far been somewhat faster compared to Thailand (Table 8.1). The difference between the recovery experiences of the two countries becomes more significant when one goes beyond the aggregate GDP growth figure and looks at other performance indicators (Table 7.1 and Table A.2). For instance, even by mid-2000 recovery in the Thai economy continued to rely on massive public sector demand, with both private consumption and investment remaining well below pre-crisis levels. By contrast, in Malaysia the recovery process had become broad-based by late 1999, with rapid recovery in private sector consumption and investment. Unlike the situation in Malaysia, problems in the financial sector still remained a major source of uncertainty in Thailand. Even by early 2000, the NPL ratio of the Thai financial system continued to remain stubbornly high (nearly 40 per cent), and the volume of real outstanding credit was still falling. Reflecting

Table 8.1 *GDP growth in Malaysia, Korea and Thailand (percentage change from one year before), 1995–99*

	Korea	Malaysia	Thailand
1995	8.9	9.8	8.9
1996	6.8	10.0	5.9
1997	5.0	7.5	–1.8
1998	–5.8	–7.5	–10.4
1999	10.7	5.4	4.0
2000[1]	6.0	5.8	4.2
1998Q1	–3.6	–3.1	–9.0
1998Q2	–8.0	–5.2	–12.7
1998Q3	–8.1	–10.9	–13.2
1998Q4	–5.3	–10.3	–6.6
1999Q1	5.4	–1.3	0.2
1999Q2	10.8	4.1	2.6
1999Q3	12.8	8.2	7.4
1999Q4	13.0	10.6	6.5

Note: 1. Official growth forecast.

Source: Asia Recovery Information Centre database, Asian Development Bank (*www.aric.adb.org*).

mostly continuing financial sector weaknesses, recovery of the share market in Thailand began to falter from about early 2000, compared to an impressive continuing recovery of the Malaysian share market. As a result of share market-related capital outflows, Thailand's foreign reserve levels had begun to be depleted by this time, causing policy concerns about the sustainability of recovery (Siamwalla, 2000).

But one should not read too much meaning into a simple statistical comparison of this nature. It ignores the important fact that the economies under consideration are vastly different in terms of the sources of vulnerability to the crisis as well as the nature of the economic structure that determines flexibility of adjustment to a crisis. Put simply, details differ in important ways from one country to another, and readily available performance indicators do not capture these differences (Cooper, 1999a). An inter-country comparison can, therefore, yield meaningful inferences only if economic adjustment under alternative policies is carefully studied while placing emphasis on fundamental differences in economic structures and original sources of vulnerability to the crisis. A comprehensive comparative analysis of this nature is beyond the scope of this volume.[1]

In any case, in examining the outcome of the Malaysian experiment, there is little justification for centring the analysis on the issue of *whether Malaysia has performed better than the IMF-programme countries*. As we have discussed in Chapter 6, the September 1998 policy U-turn in Malaysia was basically a policy choice made in desperation. There is no evidence to suggest that Malaysian policy makers anticipated this move to generate a *superior* outcome. Moreover, the almost unanimous view of the critics at the time was that Malaysia's non-conventional approach was doomed to fail. The appropriate question is therefore whether this unorthodox policy shift helped Malaysia to recover *as fast as the IMF programme countries*.

We have seen that Malaysia has recorded an impressive recovery, which is at least as good as, if not better than, that of Thailand. The purpose of this chapter is to broaden our understanding about the way capital controls were instrumental in achieving this recovery. Our approach is to examine whether the original expectations (mostly negative) about the fate of the reform programme were in fact consistent with the actual experience.

MONETARY POLICY AUTONOMY

A major doubt about the effectiveness of capital controls as a crisis management tool related to presumably ample scope for avoidance and evasion, which can negate the expected monetary policy autonomy (see, for example, Hale, 1998; Hill, 1998; Edwards, 1999a). The general argument was that the more extensive are trade and investment links, the more difficult and costly it is to control capital account transactions, because of the multiplication in the number of arbitrage possibilities that arise in the course of normal business.

The problem with this argument is that it is based on a misleading mixing of 'placing funds abroad retail', by manipulating current account transactions, and 'exporting capital wholesale' (Williamson, 1993, p. 36). There is ample evidence from both developed and developing countries that capital controls are in fact effective in substantially reducing, if not preventing, capital flows of the latter type, in particular placement abroad of institutional savings (De Gregorio *et al.*, 1998; Radelet and Sachs, 1998).

The evidence from capital controls in Malaysia is consistent with this evidence. Controls seem to have helped to lower interest rates and to encourage a revival of domestic consumption and investment without precipitating capital flights. Following the imposition of capital control measures the foreign reserve position began to move in tandem with the surplus in the current account. Total foreign exchange reserves, which remained around $20 billion from the third quarter of 1997, surpassed the pre-crisis level of $30 billion by the end of 1999 (Table 7.1). The 'errors and omission' item in the balance of payments, which is widely considered to be a convenient indicator of 'unofficial' capital flows (Dooley, 1995; Gavin *et al.*, 1996), in fact shrank following the imposition of capital controls (Table 5.1). As foreign exchange controls were carefully aimed only at short-term investment flows, and trade and FDI-related transactions remained liberal, the policy shift did not result in the emergence of a black market for foreign exchange.

The effectiveness of capital controls in bringing in expected monetary policy autonomy is evident from the dramatic turnaround in the differential between domestic and international interest rates in Malaysia following the imposition of these controls (Figure 8.1). The differential remained positive and varied in the range of 0.6 per cent to 2 per cent during the period before the onset of the crisis. Then it increased, reaching a peak of 5 per cent at the height of the crisis in mid-1998. Following the imposition of capital controls in September 1998, it tended to decline, entering the negative territory by March 1999. From then the differential has remained around –2.5 per cent with little monthly fluctuation. Both the dramatic decline in the differential and its remarkable stability in recent months clearly attest to the effectiveness of controls in insulating domestic interest rate from international financial market developments.

A comparison of the behaviour of the interest rate differential among Korea, Thailand and Malaysia reveals some interesting patterns (Figure 8.1). In the two former countries the differential widened at a much faster rate than in Malaysia in the immediate aftermath of the crisis. This difference seems to reflect at least two factors. Firstly, and perhaps more importantly, Korea and Thailand resorted to a high interest rate policy (as part of the IMF programmes) to defend the exchange rate. In Malaysia, despite the initial declared policy commitment to contractionary monetary policy, implementation was half-hearted, to say the least (see Chapter 5). Secondly, given the high foreign exchange exposure resulting from much greater accumulation of short-term foreign debt in the lead-up to the crisis, foreign exchange market participants would have attached higher risk premia to the won and baht than to the ringgit.

The interest rate differentials of Korea and Thailand began to decline from about the second quarter of 1998. This is consistent with the gradual stabilization of the exchange rate that was brought about by improved market confidence gained through firm commitment to a reform process under the IMF surveillance, coupled with massive build-up of foreign reserves and, subsequently, the emergence of some signs of recovery. In Malaysia the interest rate differential continued to remain high (by historical standards) until the third quarter of 1998, reflecting continued policy uncertainly. Fol-

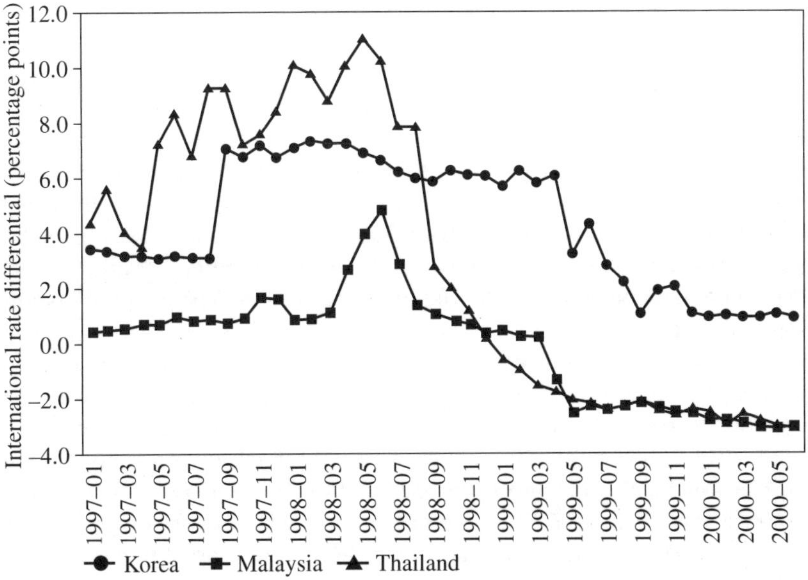

Note: Domestic money market rate used for each of the three countries is Malaysia: three-month Treasury bill rate; Thailand: three-month repurchase rate on government bonds in the inter-bank market; Korea: 91-day beneficial certificate rate. The three-month Treasury bill rate in the USA is used as a proxy for international money market rate.

Source: Bank Negara Malaysia, *Monthly Statistical Bulletin* and IMF, *International Financial Statistics* (various issues).

Figure 8.1 Differential between domestic and international money market interest rates in Malaysia, Korea and Thailand, January 1997–June 2000

lowing the introduction of the new policy package in September, it has declined in stages in line with increasing monetary policy relaxation.

Interestingly, despite continuous decline, Korea's interest rate differential continued to remain higher than that of Thailand and Malaysia. Moreover, from about late 1999, there has been a striking similarity between Thailand and Malaysia in terms of the average level of the differentials. An in-depth analysis of these intriguing patterns is beyond the scope of this study, but there is evidence to suggest that the nature of capital account regimes in the three countries seems to provide reasonable explanation. Unlike Thailand, Korea embarked on a process of further opening of domestic financial markets to foreign capital inflows (Kim, 2000). By contrast, contrary to the popular perception, capital controls have remained an important feature of

Thailand's reform process ever since the onset of the crisis (Nidhiprabha and Warr, 2000, pp.108–9).

Shortly after the onset of the crisis, the Bank of Thailand introduced strict controls on all transactions of commercial banks' sales of foreign exchange, requiring supporting documents to make sure that all private transfers were genuine and unrelated to capital flight. Following the collapse of the baht to a record low level in early 1998, the Bank of Thailand put a limit on the amount of credit denominated in baht which each financial institution could provide for non-residents. On 5 October, a maximum limit of 50 million baht was imposed on borrowing by a foreign investor for a local financial institution, unless backed by genuine trade and investment in Thailand. Although milder than those in Malaysia, these controls were significant enough to insulate the domestic money markets from short-term capital mobility. In addition to these measures, the Bank of Thailand seems to have resorted extensively to moral suasion to prevent large capital outflows through the banking system over the past three years. All in all, the popular characterization that 'there is a clear difference between the post-crisis reform programs pursued by Malaysia and Thailand in that Malaysia resorted to capital controls whereas Thailand did not … is not strictly correct' (Nidhiprabha and Warr, 2000, p. 108).

BANKING AND CORPORATE RESTRUCTURING

The breathing space provided by capital controls, exchange rate stability and the resultant monetary policy autonomy was instrumental in speedy implementation of banking and corporate restructuring. By mid-2000, *Danaharta* had successfully carved out bad debts to the tune of $12 billion (equivalent to 42.2 per cent of total NPLs) from the entire banking system. Through the operation of *Danamodal*, the capital base of the banking system had been raised much higher than the international (BIS) requirement. The Corporate Debt Restructuring Committee had resolved bad debt problems of 25 firms with loans totalling $4.7 billion, and was resolving another 26 cases with debt amounting to $4.3 billion.

As a result of the support provided by low interest rates and rapid recovery in containing NPL growth, performance of the banking and corporate sectors improved at a faster rate than originally envisaged. Consequently, *Danamodal* required considerably less funding than originally envisaged. *Danaharta* had ceased purchasing non-performing loans by mid-2000 and entered the 'work out' phase of managing the acquired assets.

Many feared that, under the *Danaharta*/*Danamodal* programme, baling out of the well connected would come at the expense of the poor and the middle class using the printing press backed by capital controls. This suspicion has given way to a virtual general consensus among Malaysia observers that the shelter has been successfully used to carry out the most effective and far-reaching financial system clean-up among the crisis countries. The programme is considered to have been more effective and fair than many similar efforts in the region, notably those of Thailand and Indonesia, but also that of Korea (Ogus, 2000). *The Economist*, in a dramatic reversal from previous pessimistic views, recently commended the Malaysian banking and corporate restructuring effort in the following words:

> In Malaysia there are doubts about the government's handling of debtors; well connected ones have emerged in better shape than some analysts think they should have done. But the government's success in holding down the level of bad debts, and in cleaning up the ones that did emerge, has been undeniable. That is one reason why Malaysia's short-term prospects are so good. (*The Economists* 2000, p. 74)

Carving out of bad debts and recapitalization of weak banks improved the lending capacity of the banking system. This, coupled with easing of monetary policy on the back of capital controls, lowered the cost of credit in the

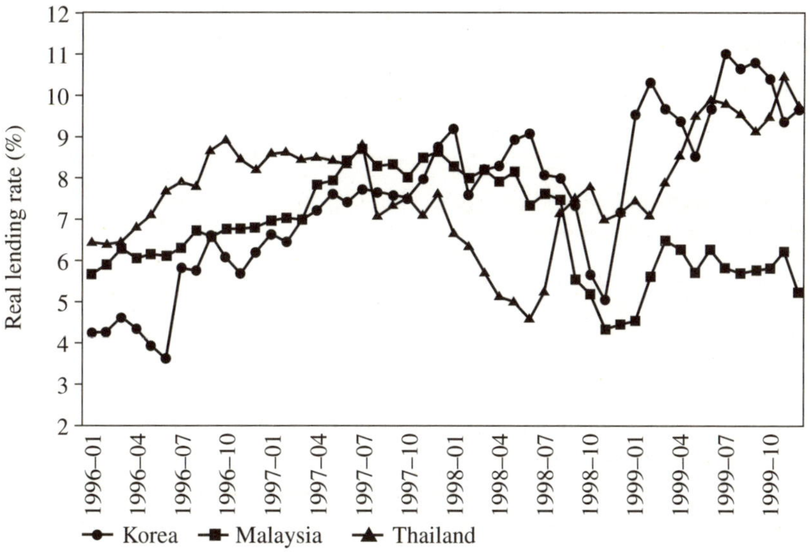

Source: Data compiled from IMF, *International Financial Statistics* (various issues).

Figure 8.2 Average real bank lending rates in Korea, Malaysia and Thailand, January 1996–December 1999

Table 8.2 Malaysian banking system:[1] *indicators of lending performance, 1995–2000*

	Outstanding loans	Outstanding loans net of NPLs[2]	NPLs as % of total outstanding loans (a)[2]	(b)[3]	Real bank credit (annual change,%)[4]
1995	260	246	5.5	—	22.5
1996	337	325	3.7	—	23.2
1997	611	586	4.1	—	23.8
1998	694	642	7.5	—	–4.0
1999	719	672	6.6	—	–2.0
1998Q1	548	510	7.0	—	12.6
1998Q2	594	541	8.9	—	4.5
1998Q3	639	587	8.1	12.8	–1.1
1998Q4	694	642	7.5	13.4	–4.1
1999Q1	659	607	7.9	13.0	–6.9
1999Q2	673	620	7.9	12.4	–1.2
1999Q3	680	628	7.7	12.0	0.3
1999Q4	719	672	6.6	11.1	1.3
2000Q1	733	685	6.5	10.9	0.3
2000Q2	737	689	6.5	10.5	0.6

Notes:
1. Commercial banks, finance companies and merchant banks.
2. NPLs classified using a 6-month default period.
3. NPLs classified using a 3-month default period.
4. Growth of loans extended by the banking system adjusted for CPI inflation.

Source: Compiled from Bank Negara Malaysia, *Monthly Bulletin of Statistics* (various issues).

economy. The average lending rate of commercial banks declined from 12.2 per cent in October 1998 to 7.8 per cent by the end of 1999. Figure 8.2 depicts the behaviour of real bank deposit rates in Korea, Malaysia and Thailand. Again the impact of the Malaysian approach to crisis management on the domestic financial scene is vividly demonstrated. Real lending rate in Malaysia has been persistently lower, and remarkably stable from about the second quarter of 1999, compared to the other two countries. In Korea and Thailand, the rates declined from about mid-1988 to the second quarter of 1999 and then started to increase.

Reflecting the combined effect of these factors, both loan approvals and disbursements, which contracted throughout 1998, began to recover from early 1999 (Table 8.2). The restoration of bank lending seems to have been a factor behind the broad-based recovery. A moribund credit market essentially constrains recovery by discouraging credit-worthy businesses which would have been willing to spend more if they had had access to credit.[2] Moreover, as Krueger and Tornell (1999) have demonstrated in the context of the Mexican economy following the 1994 crisis, continuing credit crunch caused by delayed banking restructuring could act as a major constraint on firms in the non-traded goods sectors (which are normally the most affected by the crisis) and small firms in the traded goods sector, which normally do not have favoured access to limited domestic lending sources or to foreign borrowing despite improved profitability of operation. This could lead to a lopsided recovery process involving predominantly traded goods industries dominated by large (mostly export-oriented) firms. Malaysia seems to have avoided this 'Mexican' syndrome through early action in the sphere of banking restructuring.

FIXED EXCHANGE RATE AND INTERNATIONAL COMPETITIVENESS

Fixing of the exchange rate at 3.80 ringgit per US dollar as part of the capital control-based recovery package was originally considered by many observers as a risky strategy. The new fixed rate was implemented as part of a policy package whose prime aim was to inflate the economy artificially through fiscal pump priming and expansionary monetary policy. Thus there was a possibility that domestic inflation might result in real exchange rate appreciation, hindering recovery in tradable (both import-competing and export-oriented) sectors in the economy.

By the time of writing (September 2000), two years following the policy shift, there were no indications of this pessimistic scenario unfolding. As noted, domestic inflation continued to remain low, reflecting mostly excess production capacity in the economy. Continued sizable presence of migrant workers in the country also helped keep a lid on wage growth (Kassim, 2000). Low inflation and the fixed exchange rate have continued to assist the traded goods sectors in the economy through improved international competitiveness.

Figure 8.3 compares the real exchange rate behaviour in Malaysia with that of Thailand and Korea. It is evident that Korea and Thailand began to experience persistent appreciation in the real exchange rate from about the third quarter of 1999. By contrast, the real exchange rate in Malaysia contin-

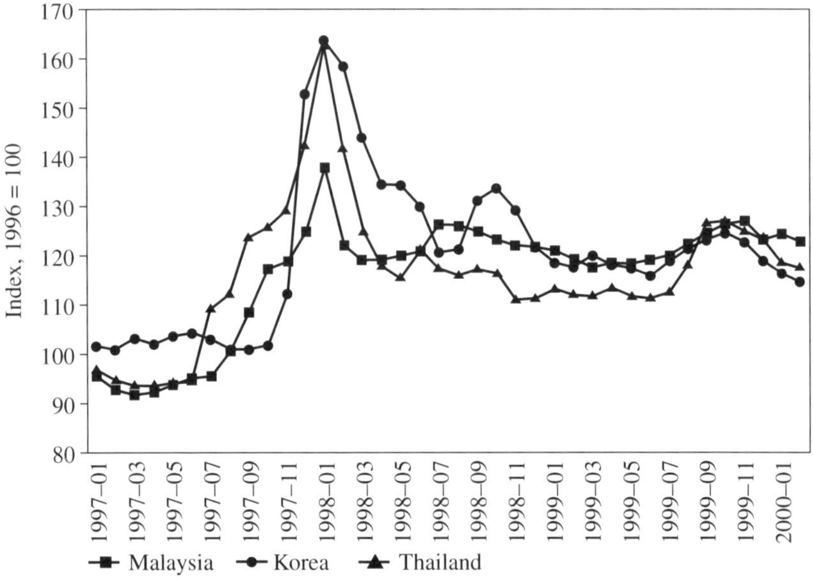

Note: * Export-weighted producer price index of the ten major export destination countries in domestic currency relative to domestic producer price. For details on methodology, see Chapter 4.

Source: Compiled from IMF, *International Financial Statistics* and *Direction of World Trade* data tapes, and BNM, *Monthly Statistical Bulletin*, Kuala Lumpur.

Figure 8.3 Real exchange rate index: Korea, Malaysia and Thailand (1996 = 100), January 1997–February 2000*

ued to experience a mild depreciation, with relatively low periodic fluctuations. In Thailand and Korea, domestic price trends have been similar to those in Malaysia, yet appreciation of the nominal exchange rate propelled by the resurgence of short-term capital flows seems to have caused an appreciation of the real exchange rate (Tables 7.1, A.3 and A.4).

As Malaysian policy makers have openly admitted, continued reliance on a fixed rate is neither feasible nor desirable. So far Bank Negara Malaysia has not confronted the 'impossible trinity' (see Chapter 6, note 5), for two reasons. Firstly, despite huge current account surpluses, base-money stock still remains below the pre-crisis level. Secondly, as noted, domestic inflation still remains low. These features of the economic landscape are likely to change rapidly with continuing rapid recovery, necessitating sterilized intervention in a big way to maintain macroeconomic stability, provided the authorities do not want to compromise on exchange rate stability.

Indications are that BNM has already started sterilization operations; 'sterilization debt' (BNM's liabilities on commercial banks) increased from almost zero by late 1998 to nearly 20 per cent of GDP by early 2000 (Nellor, 2000, Chart 3). As portfolio inflows have already begun to accelerate from early 2000, efficacy of sterilized intervention in combining domestic macroeconomic stability with a seemingly undervalued exchange rate is going to become increasingly difficult.

IMPACT ON FOREIGN DIRECT INVESTMENT

Many commentators expressed the fear that capital controls would hamper the economic recovery by adversely affecting foreign direct investment in Malaysia (Hiebert, 1999; Miller, 1999; Hale, 1998; Hill, 1998). It was argued that a policy measure that constitutes a significant departure from a long-standing commitment to economic openness could certainly have an adverse impact on the general investment climate of the country. Moreover, in Malaysia, the decision to impose controls appeared so sudden and arbitrary that it called into question the general credibility of the government's whole framework for foreign investment. However, whether this would translate into a significant reduction of FDI flows remained debatable at the time. The pessimistic view was based on a false aggregation of FDI with portfolio investment and short-term bank credits. It ignored the time-honoured dictum in the balance of payments theory that, 'in terms of underlying determinants of mobility, long term investment (FDI) is quite different from "hot money"' (Meade, 1951, p. 298). FDI flows are determined by long-term considerations governing international production decisions of MNEs, not by financial panics and related short-term economic changes, which underpin hot money movement. Therefore, regarding the external economic policy of a country, what is primarily important for attracting FDI is a firm commitment to the maintenance of an open current account (Bhagwati, 1998a).

The findings of a questionnaire survey of the impact of capital controls on manufacturing firms, conducted by MIER in late 1998, are basically consistent with the latter view (MIER, 1999).[3] The survey failed to detect any significant impact of new capital controls on operational and investment decisions of both local and foreign firms. The majority (about 60 per cent) of firms indicated political stability, rather than capital controls, as the most important criterion for investing in Malaysia in the future. Over 85 per cent of firms (90 per cent of firms with FDI) disclosed plans to maintain investment levels in the next one to three years.

The prevailing view that capital controls adversely affected FDI flows to Malaysia is based on a comparison of Malaysia's post-crisis experience with that of Thailand and Korea. According to official data, during the post-crisis period FDI inflows to Thailand and Korea have indeed increased at a faster rate than those coming to Malaysia (Table 8.3). However, this is not a correct comparison and needs to be treated cautiously because in Thailand and Korea acquisition by foreign companies of assets or equity of domestic companies has been a major component of foreign capital inflows during this period. Despite the severity of the downturn, corporate distress was far less widespread in Malaysia than elsewhere, and there were simply fewer bargain assets. For instance, during the period from 1 January to 15 April 1999, capital inflows relating to these activities amounted to US$27 billion in

Table 8.3 Foreign direct investment[1] in Korea, Malaysia and Thailand (US$ million), 1995–2000Q2

	Korea	Malaysia	Thailand
1995	1 776	9 294	2 068
1996	2 325	11 951	2 336
1997	2 844	12 536	3 746
1998	5 415	7 398	6 941
1999	7 023	7 852	5 723
1997Q1	624	2 833	645
1997Q2	791	4 745	842
1997Q3	611	3 101	1 222
1997Q4	819	2 215	1 037
1998Q1	505	1 658	1 870
1998Q2	1 168	1 634	2 628
1998Q3	2 162	1 357	1 249
1998Q4	1 582	2 787	1 031
1999Q1	1 407	1 546	1 004
1999Q2	1 819	2 634	2 203
1999Q3	2 607	2 561	1 173
1999Q4	1 730	1 111	1 344
2000Q1	283	1 507	797
2000Q2	1 788	1 209	651

Note: 1. Gross inflow of equity and inter-company loans.

Source: Korea and Thailand: IMF, *International Financial Statistics* (line 77*bed*) (various issues); Malaysia: Bank Negara Malaysia, electronic database, Tables VIII.13 and VIII.14 (*http://bnm.gov.my*).

Korea and US$20 billion in Thailand, compared to US$2 billion in Malaysia (Goad, 1999, p. 38). Unlike Korea and Thailand, Malaysia did not resort to promoting acquisition or takeover by foreign companies as part of the continuing process of corporate and banking restructuring.

Moreover, accordingly to the FDI classification system adopted by Bank Negara Malaysia in its balance of payments accounts, 'purchase of existing plant and equipment' by foreigners is treated as 'changes of ownership', not as 'new investment'. Because of this (sound) accounting practice, whatever takeovers have happened are not reflected in official FDI figures, whereas in Thailand and Korea the value of these deals is captured in FDI data, together with 'true' investment (Ogus, 2000).

When allowance is made for these considerations, the decline in FDI flows to Malaysia may be treated as part of the general decline in investment in the country following the onset of the crisis. This view is supported by the data on proposed and approved investment reported in Table 8.4. Note that decline in both proposed and approved investment over the past two years is common to both foreign and domestic investment. If anything, domestic private investment has declined at a much faster rate than FDI.

Table 8.4 Investment applications and approvals in Malaysian manufacturing (US$ billion), 1996–9

	1996	1997	1998	1999
Applications	16.7	12.2	5.1	3.8
FDI	7.0	5.1	3.2	1.6
Local	9.7	7.1	2.9	1.2
Approvals	13.6	9.2	6.7	4.4
FDI	6.8	4.1	3.3	3.6
Private domestic	6.8	5.1	3.4	0.8

Source: National Economic Action Council, Malaysia (*http:/neac.gov.my*).

IMPACT ON PORTFOLIO INVESTMENT

Would portfolio investors ignore Malaysia forever as a punishment for its recalcitrant act? This question is important because, despite the disruptive role they played in the crisis context, foreign portfolio inflows have important positive effects, when harnessed in an appropriate macroeconomic setting. They contribute to expansion in domestic investment by reducing cost of equity capital and helping firms to reduce their reliance on bank-based financial intermediation (Williamson, 1999b).

When the capital controls were first introduced (and even after the new levy was introduced in February 1999) many observers were concerned about potential massive outflows of short-term foreign debt and portfolio investment after 1 September 1999. However, the ending of the one-year moratorium turned out to be a non-event. Total net portfolio capital outflow in the fourth quarter of 1999 amounted to only US$2.2 billion, compared to a total stock of about $10 billion potentially movable foreign portfolio investment remaining in the country at the time the restriction was lifted (IMF, 1999a, p. 98). Net outflows turned out to be positive by mid-January 2000 and the first quarter of the year recorded a total net inflow of US$2.4 billion (Table 8.5). This investment pattern seems to suggest that investors do not find it difficult to factor in the new profit tax on portfolio investment, as ground rules are now more transparent in a context where signs of economic recovery are already clearly visible. The resurgence of portfolio flows also may have come

Table 8.5 Net portfolio capital flows (US$ million), March 1999–May 2000

	Net portfolio inflow US$ million
1999 March	25.3
1999 April	126.3
1999 May	478.5
1999 June	396.6
1999 July	191.2
1999 August	–484.1
1999 September	–1 076.3
1999 October	–638.6
1999 November	74.7
1999 December	–181.8
2000 January	915.4
2000 February	1 131.5
2000 March	416
2000 April	–205
2000 May	140

Source: Estimated from weekly data on net outstanding balances on flow of funds through external accounts published in the website of the National Economic Action Council, Malaysia (*http://neac.gov.my/figures/flow.shtm*).

about because new, inexperienced investors replace the ones who have been buried, or because memories of all investors are generally short (DeLong, 1999).

Immediately after the imposition of capital controls, Morgan Stanley Capital International (MSCI), International Finance Corporation (IFC) (the investment arm of the World Bank) and Dow Jones removed Malaysia from their capital market indices. Lack of transparency in new measures at the time controls were imposed and uncertainty about future growth prospects of the economy were as much an issue as the nature of the controls themselves.[4] Following the introduction of market-friendly changes to capital controls in February 1999, and as the economy began to show clear signs of recovery, IFC and Dow Jones reinstated Malaysia in their global indices by the end of 1999. MSCI reinstated Malaysia in its global indices in June 2000.

CONCLUDING REMARKS

This chapter has examined the role of capital controls in the recovery process in Malaysia. The analysis suggests that the carefully designed capital control measures were successful in providing Malaysian policy makers with a viable setting for undertaking Keynesian reflationary policies without adverse backwash effects on foreign direct investment. Controls also assisted banking and corporate restructuring by facilitating the mobilization of domestic resources and, more importantly, providing a cushion against adverse market sentiments regarding improper practices of protecting favoured companies and corporations. There is no evidence to suggest that controls on volatile short-term capital flows have had an adverse impact on foreign direct investment. Nor is there evidence that portfolio investors will desert Malaysia as a punishment for the way they were treated in the context of the crisis.

NOTES

1. Apart from usual time and resource constraints facing any solo research project of this nature, the time is not ripe for an in-depth comparative case study. We have to wait until the recovery process becomes well rooted and policy responses are well embedded in economic data.
2. To place the discussion in historical perspective, it is pertinent to mention that the failure to take timely action to reactivate the banking system is widely cited as a prime reason for the persistence of the Great Depression for so long in the USA and a number of other countries (Kindleberger, 1986, pp.94–6; Krugman, 1999b, p. 75; Hall and Ferguson, 1998, ch. 8).
3. The 135 firms accounting for over 60 per cent of total manufacturing output in the country

responded to the questionnaire. Of these firms, 77 were with foreign capital participation (wholly foreign-owned: 33; joint ventures: 44) and 58 fully locally owned.

4. It is pertinent to mention here that the imposition in the early 1990s of capital controls on repatriation of existing capital that involved a lock-up of five years did not lead to an exclusion of the Chilean market from these indices. Presumably this was because transparency was not an issue in Chile (Merrill Lynch, 1999).

9. Conclusion

When the floating of the Thai baht sparked off the financial crisis in East Asia in July 1997, a first look at the Malaysian economy would have hardly raised suspicion that it would succumb to a Thai-like financial crisis. The general performance indicators of the Malaysian economy were very favourable, at virtual full employment for the previous six years, with modest inflation. The country's foreign currency sovereign credit rating was an A+, in the same league as Hong Kong. It also had a continuing high inflow of long-term capital, as contrasted to Thailand's short-term capital inflows. With a very low non-performing loan ratio and a seemingly high capital adequacy ratio, the Malaysian banking system looked fairly robust. In terms of political stability and policy continuity, Malaysia fared much better than Thailand and other crisis economies. Yet the crisis hit Malaysia with ferocity.

What happened to Malaysia? Did it simply fall victim to a wild speculative attack in the wake of the Thai crisis or were there some fundamental weaknesses in the pre-crisis Malaysian economy that made it vulnerable to the Thai contagion?

When the Malaysian macroeconomic performance prior to the crisis is closely examined in the light of the literature on currency crises, there is considerable evidence that Malaysia succumbed to the Thai contagion because its economy had developed considerable vulnerability to a speculative attack. Malaysia had accumulated massive short-term capital inflows (mostly in the form of portfolio capital) following capital market liberalization initiatives in the early 1990s, which coincided with the rapid spread of global capital to emerging market economies. These capital flows interacted with notable slippage in domestic macroeconomic policy to make the country vulnerable to speculative attack. By the mid-1990s, three clear signs of vulnerability were visible: a significant appreciation of the real exchange rate, rapid depletion of foreign exchange reserves relative to accumulated mobile foreign capital, and some fundamental weaknesses in the financial system. The seeming success of an economy and the admiration of markets and media for its managers was no guarantee that the economy was immune to financial crises

The Malaysian experience has been interpreted to imply that, in the presence of volatile capital, a country can succumb to an international financial crisis, even if it had faithfully followed the conventional policy advocacy on sequencing of capital account liberalization (Bhagwati, 1998b; Furman and Stiglitz, 1998; Radelet and Sachs, 1998). Our analysis of policy trends and economic performance in the pre-crisis Malaysian economy does not support this view.

It is true that capital account opening in Malaysia followed current account opening. But by the time these reforms were implemented there was a clear departure from conventional macroeconomic prudence. The opening of domestic capital markets to equity investors was not appropriately combined with initiatives to improve corporate governance. Massive bank lending fuelled by the public investment boom and the dramatic expansion in share trading created a highly leveraged economy. This, coupled with a share market bubble in which foreign institutional investors played an important role, set the stage for a speculative attack on the currency and the subsequent economic collapse.

Closer regulation and monitoring of private sector foreign currency borrowing by the central bank prevented accumulation of excessive foreign borrowing in Malaysia, unlike the case of Thailand, Korea and Indonesia. However, this favourable feature of the policy environment was overwhelmed by haphazard capital account liberalization, in a context of significant departure from the conventional fiscal and monetary prudence associated with a 'big push' public investment programme. The erosion of policy autonomy historically enjoyed by the central bank as part of the growth euphoria was reflected in a massive credit build-up in the economy and significant deterioration in the quality of banks' asset portfolios.

While the initial currency collapse in mid-1997 was consistent with weak economic fundamentals, the depth of the economic slump that followed was aggravated by the uniquely tricky political economy of Malaysia. The initial response of the Malaysian government to the outbreak of the currency crisis was one of denial. Given the perceived soundness of economic fundamentals, and the initial success of BNM in repelling speculators in May, Malaysian policy makers acted as if the country was in a different economic league from that of Thailand and Indonesia. The end result of policy fragility was an outright financial and economic collapse. This set the stage for a radical policy shift.

Some commentators have referred to the imposition of controls on capital outflow by the Malaysian government as *a ritualistic locking of the barn door after the horse was stolen*. This is a misleading remark because the purpose of controls was to set the stage for monetary expansion by preventing outflow of funds, both local and foreign-owned, in response to lowering of the domestic interest rate relative to world market rates. The potential threat of such outflow was much greater in Malaysia than in the other crisis-hit countries because of the pivotal role played by the Singapore money market as a convenient alternative to the domestic market for the Malaysian investor.

Malaysia has certainly survived dire predictions made by many observers at the time it embarked on a radical policy path in October 1998. Once the Malaysian authorities decided to deviate from the IMF route and follow the conventional Keynesian recipe for crisis management, capital control seems to have provided a conducive setting for the effective pursuance of such policies. The new policy has prevented massive capital outflow and permitted the sustaining of a significant interest rate differential with the rest of the world. Against the popular perception that short-term capital flows cannot be controlled in a highly trade-oriented economy, the Malaysian evidence suggests that these flows can be effectively regulated (at least at the margin), provided the controls are specifically aimed at capital account transactions.

So far the fixed exchange rate has helped the recovery process by preventing premature exchange rate appreciation as part of improved market sentiments about the prospects of recovery. However, as the recovery process gathers momentum, it will become difficult to maintain international competitiveness without shifting over to a more flexible rate.

There is no clear evidence to suggest that controls on short-term capital flows have adversely affected Malaysia's image as a favourable location for foreign direct investment. On the contrary, there is anecdotal evidence that foreign investors, particularly those involved in export-oriented production, favour capital controls and the fixed exchange rate as sources of stability in the investment climate. The time-honoured dictum (and yet one much neglected in the current debate on crisis management) that the long-term investment is determined by quite different factors compared to 'hot money' movements is reconfirmed by the Malaysian experiment. Foreign portfolio investors have not completely deserted Malaysia either. The lesson here is that the use of capital control is unlikely to have an adverse lingering effect on foreign portfolio investment, provided timely steps are taken to introduce greater flexibility and transparency to the regulatory mechanism and the reform process brings about speedy economic recovery.

One can still dispute the argument that controls have played a 'special role' in delivering a superior recovery outcome for Malaysia (compared to the IMF-programme countries) for want of counterfactuals. However, the fact remains that the new policy measures enabled Malaysia to achieve recovery while minimizing social costs and economic disruptions associated with a more market-oriented path to reform. This itself is a significant achievement because maintaining social harmony is an overriding concern (quite apart from economic efficiency considerations) of economic policy making in ethically diverse Malaysia (Crouch, 1998). Even if the bloody racial riots of 1969 are ignored as a distant event, the ethnic tension created by the modest economic downturn in the mid-1980s cannot be entirely overlooked.

Some argue that Malaysia's recovery would have been even faster under an IMF-centred policy package, because, unlike Thailand, Korea and Indonesia, it really did not have a serious crisis to begin with (*The Economist*, 1999; Lim, 1999). This view is primarily based on Malaysia's relatively low foreign debt levels. It ignores the explosive mix of share market bubble and domestic credit boom that had developed in Malaysia in the lead-up to the crisis.[1] In any case, that the severity of a speculative attack on the currency of a country is proportional to the degree of vulnerability is not a convincing argument. If foreign lenders suspect an impending crisis, they do not expect to be told how serious the problem may become. They will simply withdraw their funds as rapidly as possible, thus turning a suspected financial problem into a financial rout (Cooper, 1998).

An important issue that we have not addressed in this volume is the long-term growth implications of crisis management behind closed doors. If the Malaysian authorities have made use of the breathing space provided by capital controls to rescue companies and banks that were rendered illiquid by the financial panic (unable to roll over short-term credit) but were otherwise viable, then the underlying growth prospects of the economy will remain intact. Alternatively, if bail-outs assisted inefficient (mostly politically linked) firms whose insolvency was hastened by the high interest rates and lower aggregate demand, then growth prospects would have been impaired. Such a rescue operation may also induce moral hazard by encouraging firms or banks to continue engaging in risky acts, in the hope that they will be rescued in the event of similar future crises.

There is indeed anecdotal evidence of inappropriate rescue operations (Ariff, 1999; Yap, 1999). But whether these costly practices are unique to the capital control-based crisis management in Malaysia is a debatable issue. Similar concerns have been raised relating to banking and corporate restructuring processes in Thailand, Korea and Indonesia – countries that are riding the crisis without explicit capital controls. Moreover, one can reasonably argue (along the lines of Krueger and Tornell, 1999, for instance) that economic gains associated with the speedy implementation of banking and corporate restructuring in Malaysia might have compensated significantly, if not totally, for these alleged costs.

It is pertinent to end this study with two important caveats. First, the inference that capital controls have helped crisis management in Malaysia by no means implies that Malaysia's radical policy shift should be treated as a ready-made alternative to the conventional IMF recipe adopted by other developing countries. It is of course hazardous to draw general policy lessons from the study of an individual country case. With the benefit of hindsight, one can reasonably argue that a number of factors specific to Malaysia as well as to the timing of policy reforms may have significantly conditioned the actual policy outcome. As noted, thanks to long-standing prudential controls on foreign borrowing, Malaysia succumbed to the crisis with limited foreign debt exposure. With a vast domestic revenue base and ready access to 'captive' domestic financial sources (in particular the Employees Provident Fund (EPF) and the oil-rich Petronas), the Malaysian government was relatively better placed than perhaps any other crisis country to make a decisive departure from the conventional, IMF-centred approach to crisis management. The implementation of new controls was also greatly aided by a well-developed banking system, which was able to perform most of the new functions smoothly in the normal course of its business.

Secondly, the inference that capital controls have helped crisis management in Malaysia by no means implies that these controls should be retained after the economy recovers. Despite its underlying logic in a crisis context, the new strategy is costly in terms of long-term growth implications. The rationale behind the imposition of capital controls is to avert a painful economic collapse and to provide a conducive setting for the implementation of the required adjustment policies, in particular banking and corporate restructuring. The danger is that the complacence induced by possible temporary recovery through expansionary policies may lead to postponement of long-term structural reforms, and thus to long-term economic deterioration. Moreover, any form of market intervention of this nature involves economic costs associated with bureaucratic controls and related rent-seeking activities. Prolonged use of controls is likely to compound these costs. The greatest challenge for the Malaysian policy makers is, therefore, to strengthen the domestic financial system and to regain macroeconomic prudence, which sadly dissipated during the period of growth euphoria in the early 1990s, in order to set the stage for an orderly exiting from capital controls.

NOTE

1. Interestingly, on these grounds, the international financier George Soros (1998, ch. 7) treats the economic situation in Malaysia in the lead-up to the crisis as untenable as (if not more untenable than) that in Korea, Thailand and Indonesia.

APPENDIX

Table A.1 Malaysia: a chronology of crisis, policy response and recovery

1997	
14–15 May	Bank of Thailand intervened to defend baht from attack by speculators.
2 July	Bank of Thailand abandoned the long-standing peg of the baht to the US dollar. The new market-determined rate (US$/baht = 30) reflected about 18 per cent depreciation against the US dollar.
8 July	Bank Negara Malaysia (BNM) (the Malaysian central bank) intervened aggressively to defend the ringgit, boosting the currency to a high of 2.5100 after a low of 2.5240.
14 July	BNM gave up the defence of the ringgit after unsuccessfully defending it by jacking up interest rates to 50 per cent and spending an estimated US$3 billion. The ringgit plunged to a 33-month low.
24 July	Malaysian ringgit hit 38-month low of 2.653 to the US dollar, and Prime Minister Mahathir launched a bitter attack on 'rogue speculators'.
26 July	Dr Mahathir named George Soros as the man responsible for the attack on the ringgit.
30 July	In response to a question raised by a news reporter (at a news conference after a cabinet meeting) about the possible use of exchange controls, Dr Mahathir responded that 'the cabinet discussed it and will take action … but I can't tell you'. This intensified the speculative run on the ringgit.
4 August	Bank Negara Malaysia instructed commercial banks to observe a US$2 million limit on non-commercial ringgit offer-side transactions with each foreign customer (with a view to insulating domestic interest rates from developments in the foreign exchange market).

Table A.1 continued

18 August	Standard and Poor's revised Malaysia's outlook to stable from positive.
21 August	Standard and Poor's Ratings affirmed long-term foreign currency and local currency ratings on Malaysia's Petroleum Nasional, Telekom and Tenaga.
28 August	KLSE banned short selling of 1000 blue-chip stocks. To discourage sales of stock, sellers were required to deliver physical share certificates to brokers before selling and settlement period was reduced from five to two days.
3 September	A plan was announced to use funds from the Employees Provident Fund (EPF) to prop up share prices, buying stocks from Malaysian shareholders, but not from foreigners, at a premium above the prevailing prices.
4 September	Ringgit broke through 3.0 against the US dollar.
	Prime Minister Mahathir announced that the implementation of a number of large public investment projects would be delayed.
5 September	Ban on short selling of KLSE-linked stocks was lifted.
15 September	KLSE introduced a share buy-back scheme to avert share price collapse.
	BNM increased the three-month intervention rate from 6 per cent to 7.55 per cent.
20 September	Addressing the World Bank and IMF Annual Meeting in Hong Kong, Dr Mahathir declared that currency trading (beyond the level needed to finance trade) was 'unnecessary, unproductive and immoral' and should therefore be made illegal. In his response, George Soros labelled him a menace to his own country.
	Some leading newspapers interpreted Mahathir's remark as an indication of a possible unilateral ban on foreign exchange transactions unrelated to foreign trade by Malaysian authorities, triggering a sell-off in the ringgit and stock market.

Table A.1 continued

	Finance Minister Anwar subsequently attempted to allay market fears by saying that there was no intention to change currency trading rules. In order to calm the markets, the finance minister made what he called a 'trick clarification' that his boss had not really meant what he said.
22 September	Ringgit went as far as 3.12 against the US dollar, the highest since at least 1971, and the KLSE composite index (KLSECI) plunged 3.5 per cent, as markets reacted to weekend remarks by Dr Mahathir suggesting restrictions on foreign currency.
24–5 September	A nationwide run on deposits of MB Finance, Malaysia's largest finance company, was sparked by rumours about its liquidity position.
25 September	Standard and Poor's Ratings revised the outlook from stable to negative on both Malaysia's 'A+' foreign currency long-term debt rating and its 'AA+' long-term local currency rating. It cited the authorities' reluctance to curb rapid credit growth and the likelihood that bank asset quality would deteriorate in the following year. The ringgit plunged from 3.06 against the US dollar to a record 3.145 at the news.
3 October	Moody's put debt and deposit ratings for Maybank and Public Bank of Malaysia under review for a possible downgrade, citing growing problems in the Malaysian economy and increasing strains on its leading banks.
17 October	Finance Minister Anwar Ibrahim unveiled the 1998 Budget, cutting infrastructure spending, with an increase in import duties and breaks for expenditures aimed at narrowing the current account deficit. Corporate tax rate was cut from 20 per cent to 28 per cent to stimulate investment. Foreign news media suggested that the steps did not suggest a nation coming to grips with its problems (tantamount to 'denial' of the gravity of the crisis and its ostensible causes).
20 November	KLSE Composite Index plunged 30 per cent in response to a controversial transaction in which United Engineer-

Table A.1 continued

	ing Malaysia (UEM), Malaysia's largest construction firm, spent nearly $700 million to buy out influential shareholders in its debt-laden (and politically connected) parent company, Renong.
29 November	Prime Minister Mahathir renewed his attack on currency speculators at the Annual Asia–Pacific Economic Cooperation (APEC) Summit in Vancouver. He stated: 'We didn't believe our ringgit fell weak, soft-kneed and collapsed. Somebody made it collapse.'
1 December	KLSECI slipped by another 3 per cent after KLSE slapped trading restrictions on five brokerages, believed to have been stuck with huge losses.
5 December	Finance Minister Anwar Ibrahim announced an austerity package. He also announced a reduction of the growth forecast for 1998 to 4–5 per cent from 7 per cent and that for 1999 to 7.5–7.7 per cent from 8.0 per cent. The package included the following: • reduction of total government expenditure by 18 per cent, • postponing of all public investment programmes indefinitely, • freezing of new share issues, • company restructuring, • reduction of ministers' salaries by 10 per cent. The media greeted this as the most important policy statement of the decade and the ringgit recovered from record 3.865 against the US dollar to 3.71, and stocks finished up 5.5 per cent on a late bounce.
22 December	Moody's lowered rating for Malaysia to A2 (still investment grade).
27 December	BNM increased its three-month intervention rate from 7.55 per cent to 8.7 per cent.
1998	
1 January	BNM reduced the period in arrears (default period) for classifying a loan as non-performing by banking institu-

Table A.1 continued

	tions from six months to three months, with a view to strengthening prudential supervision.
2 January	BNM instructed Malaysia's 39 finance companies to begin merger talks.
7 January	The National Economic Action Council (NEAC) was established as a consultative body to the cabinet to deal with the economic crisis. Daim Zainuddin, who was finance minister during the economic crisis of the late 1980s (and a close confidant of Dr Mahathir), was appointed as the executive director of NEAC.
	The same day, Finance Minister Anwar confirmed that BNM had moved to stem the slide of the ringgit.
	Ringgit touched a historic intra-day low of 4.88 per US dollar.
9 January	Government claimed sufficient foreign reserves and ruled out an IMF rescue.
16 January	Moody's put on negative review the ratings of Malaysian Banking Bhd, Bank Bumiputra Malaysia Bhd, Public Bank Bhd, and Sime Bank Bhd.
17 January	Michael Camdessus, managing director of the IMF, praised the 5 December austerity package and pointed to the need for further strengthening of policy, including monetary tightening to slow credit growth, moderate inflationary pressure and support the weakening currency. However, he confirmed the Malaysian official view that the country did not need an IMF rescue package to get it through the regional crisis.
6 February	Moody's cut Malaysia's sovereign foreign currency ratings to negative, citing potential problems in banking and corporate sectors and financial instability.
	BNM increased its three-month intervention rate from 10 per cent to 11 per cent.
9 February	Bank Negara Malaysia lowered the statutory reserve requirement (SRR) from 13.5 per cent (a rate which had

Table A.1 continued

	prevailed from 1 January 1996) to 10 per cent, to help check the extraordinary rise in bank lending rates.
16 February	The statutory reserve requirement (SRR) for commercial banks, finance companies and merchant banks was reduced from 13.5 per cent to 10 per cent of their eligible liabilities.
24 March	Bank Negara Malaysia introduced new measures for banks to shore up the capital adequacy position at the first sign of trouble. BNM also announced that three financial institutions – Bank Bumiputra, Abrar Finance and Cempaka Finance – might need to be recapitalized by a total of 782 million ringgit ($2.08 million).
23 April	The margin on bank financing of passenger cars costing RM40 000 or less was raised from 70 per cent to 85 per cent.
5 May	Prime Minister Mahathir made it clear that he disagreed with the IMF 'on the need to raise the interest rate further'.
1 June	*Pengurusan Danaharta Nasional Berhad* (the National Asset Management Company) was set up to acquire and manage NPLs of the banking institutions.
1 July	SRR was reduced from 10 per cent to 8 per cent.
23 July	NEAC launched the National Recovery Plan. Its recommendations, in particular an exchange rate system that reduces volatility, a shift away from high interest policy and easing of fiscal and monetary policy, did indicate significant departure from the conventional IMF lines, but there was no hint of an imposition of capital control.
27 July	Moody's and Standard and Poor's downgraded Malaysia's long-term foreign currency rating.
28 July	The 85 per cent financial margin applicable to bank loans for purchasing passenger cars was extended to all passenger cars and the maximum repayment period for passenger cars was abolished.
31 July	A new framework for liquidity management in banking institutions was introduced in order to enable the banking

Table A.1 continued

	institutions to manage their liquidity positions more flexibly without compromising prudential standards.
1 August	*Danamodal Nasional Berhad* (Banking Recapitalization Agency) was set up to recapitalize banking institutions.
	The Corporate Debt Restructuring Committee, a joint public and private sector steering committee, was set up to facilitate and expedite corporate debt restructuring.
3 August	BNM's market intervention rate was reduced from 11 per cent to 10.5 per cent.
10 August	BNM's market intervention rate was reduced from 10.5 per cent to 10 per cent.
17 August	BNM reduced its three-month intervention rate from 11 per cent to 9.5 per cent.
21 August	Moody's Investors Service Inc. downgraded Malaysia's sovereign credit rating by three notches, compelling the Malaysian government to cancel a planned $2 billion bond issue in Europe and the USA.
22 August	Standard & Poor's Ratings lowered Malaysia's long-term sovereign rating from 'single A minus' to 'triple B plus' and affirmed short-term foreign currency rating at 'single A –2'.
25 August	Daim Zainuddin was appointed minister of special functions to oversee the Malaysian economy. The media interpreted this as a calculated move to reduce Anwar's role in crisis management.
27 August	National accounts indicating a 6.8 per cent contraction of GDP in the second quarter of 1998 (on a year-on-year basis) were released.
	The government indicated a relaxation of monetary and fiscal policy to avoid a depression.
	BNM reduced market intervention rate from 10 per cent to 9.5 per cent and ruled out any possibility of introducing capital controls.

Table A.1 continued

28 August	The governor (Ahmad Mohamad Don) and the deputy governor (Fong Weng Phak) of BNM resigned (on policy differences, according to news media).
31 August	The Malaysian government banned overseas trading of Malaysian securities.
	KLSE announced that trading on Singapore's over-the-counter central limit order book (CLOB) market was no longer recognized.
1 September	A wide range of foreign exchange and capital controls were introduced, substantially insulating Malaysia's financial markets from external influences and effectively closing down the offshore ringgit market (see Table A.2 for details).
	SRR was reduced from 8 per cent to 6 per cent.
	The base lending rate (BLR) framework was revised to ensure a more rapid transmission of changes in monetary policy on lending rates charged by banks.
2 September	The exchange rate for the ringgit was fixed at 3.80 per US dollar, a rate which was stronger than the average rate of 4.18 for the previous two months, but significantly below its pre-crisis level of about 2.49).
	Prime Minister Mahathir sacked his deputy, Finance Minister Anwar Ibrahim, on grounds of immorality.
3 September	The liquidity–asset ratio requirement for commercial banks was reduced from 17 per cent to 15 per cent with immediate effect.
	BNM's market intervention rate was reduced from 9.5 per cent to 8 per cent.
4 September	Dr Mahathir became the acting minister of finance.
7 September	BNM relaxed ceilings on bank lending to the property sector. (Lending for the construction or purchase of residential property consisting of up to RM250 000 was exempt from the 20 per cent limit on lending to the broad property sector and the maximum margin of finance of 60 per cent was

Table A.1 continued

	abolished for the purchase of owner-occupied properties costing RM150 000 and above, the purchase of shop-houses costing RM300 000 and above which are not for the conduct of own business, and the purchase of land lots.)
	Dr Mahathir became first finance minister and Mustapa Mohamed (former minister of entrepreneur development) was appointed second finance minister.
	Tan Sri Ali Abul Hassan Sulaiman, director-general of the Economic Planning Unit, was appointed governor of BNM.
9 September	BNM instructed the banks to aim at achieving a minimum annual loan growth of 8 per cent by the end of the year.
	SRR was reduced from 6 per cent to 5 per cent.
10 September	Salomon Smith Barney was appointed finance advisor to the government and Danamodal Nasional Berhad.
16 September	SRR was reduced from 5 per cent to 4 per cent.
23 September	The ceiling on loans for the purchase of shares and unit trust funds was raised from 15 per cent to 20 per cent of total outstanding loans for commercial banks and finance companies, while leaving the ceiling on merchant banks at 30 per cent.
	The default period for classifying a loan as non-performing by banking institutions was increased from three months to six months.
28 September	Morgan Stanley Capital International removed Malaysia from its international indices (Emerging Market Free and All Country Free indices).
5 October	BNM's market intervention rate was reduced from 8 per cent to 7.5 per cent.
	Abolished 60 per cent maximum margin for financing purchase of non-owner-occupied residential properties costing RM150 000 and above, shop-houses costing RM300 000 and above, and purchase of land lots.
23 October	The 1999 Budget was unveiled by Prime Minister/First Finance Minister Mahathir. It proposed a significant fiscal

Table A.1 continued

	stimulant package involving an increase in the budget deficit as a percentage of GNP from 1.8 in 1998 to 3.2 in 1999.
9 November	BNM's market intervention rate was reduced from 7.5 per cent to 7 per cent.
20 November	The minimum monthly repayment on outstanding credit card balances was reduced from 15 per cent to 5 per cent.
	Banking institutions were instructed to establish Loan Rehabilitation Units to manage problem loans.
21 November	Hire-purchase guidelines were abolished, allowing banking institutions to determine their own hire-purchase loans.
28 November	Third quarter national accounts indicated a 8.6 per cent contraction of GDP on a year-on-year basis.
5 December	The maximum annual lending rate under the Fund for Small and Medium Industries and the Scheme for Low and Medium Cost Houses was reduced from 10 per cent to 8.5 per cent.
10 December	Malaysia received a 74 billion yen loan under Japan's Miyazawa Initiative.
30 December	The maximum finance charge payable by credit card holders was reduced to not more than 1.5 per cent per month or 18 per cent per annum from 2 per cent per month or 24 per cent per annum.
1999	
4 January	Banking institutions were instructed to achieve a minimum loan growth of 8 per cent by the end of 1999.
10 January	BNM took control of MB Finance Berhad, the biggest finance company (with assets amounting to about US$5 billion, one-quarter of total assets of all finance companies) on the grounds of weak management.
4 February	The 12-month holding rule on repatriation of foreign portfolio capital was replaced by a three-tier exit levy on the principal and profit.

Table A.1 continued

31 March	According to the BNM Annual Report for 1998, GDP contracted by 6.7 per cent in that year.
26 May	BNM raised US$1 billion through a global bond issue. The issue was oversubscribed by 300 per cent. The government highlighted this as a vindication of its non-IMF policy posture. Independent analysts ascribed the success partly to the high premium agreed on the bond issue.
23 June	KLSE all-ordinary index hit a 22-month closing high of 851.49.
29 July	BNM unveiled a plan to combine the country's 58 financial institutions (22 commercial banks, 11 merchant banks and 25 finance companies) into six large banking groups.
9 August	BNM's intervention rate was reduced from 7 per cent to 5 per cent.
12 August	Morgan Stanley Capital International announced that Kuala Lumpur Stock Exchange would be reinstated in its benchmark portfolios in February 2000, barring any financial policy reversals. (This was subsequently postponed in view of possible disruption to share market performance from the year 2000 problem.)
25 August	The authorities declared the end of recession, as GDP had grown by 4.1 per cent (year on year) in the second quarter of 1999.
21 September	The three-tier levy on repatriation of portfolio capital was replaced by a flat 10 per cent levy on profit repatriated.
16 November	Dr Mahathir announced that the number of anchor banks would be increased from six to ten or more under the proposed financial sector consolidation plan (announced on 29 July 1999).
29 November	Morgan Stanley Capital International announced that Kuala Lumpur Stock Exchange to full weighting in its benchmark portfolios on 31 May 2000.
	The ruling *Barison Nasional* (National Front) retained power with a two-thirds (yet reduced) majority at the 29 November general election.

Table A.1 continued

2000	
11 May	Dr Mahathir was re-elected as the leader of the United Malay National Organisation, the dominant party in the ruling National Front.
27 October	Profit earned from foreign portfolio investment in the country for a period of more than one year was exempted from the 10 per cent repatriation levy.
15 December	The repatriation levy on profit earned from foreign portfolio investment was abolished.

Table A.2 Malaysia: capital and exchange control measures prior to and after 1 September 1998

	Transaction	Prior to 1 September 1998	New
1	Transfers based on external accounts	Transfer between external account holders freely allowed	Transfer of any amount between external accounts requires prior approval Sources of funding external accounts are limited to: (a) proceeds from sale of ringgit instruments, securities registered in Malaysia or other assets in Malaysia, (b) salaries, wages, commissions, interests or dividends, and (c) sales of foreign currency Use of funds in accounts is limited to purchase of ringgit assets in Malaysia
2	General payments	Residents were freely allowed to make payments to non-residents for any purpose. Amounts of RM100 000 and above were permitted provided the resident did not have any domestic borrowing (if the payment was for investment abroad) or the payment was made in foreign currency (for non-trade purposes)	Residents are freely allowed to make payments to non-residents for any purpose up to RM10 000 in ringgit or foreign currency, except for imports of goods and services. Amounts exceeding RM10 000 require approval and are allowed in foreign currency only
3	Export of goods	Payments to be received in foreign currency or ringgit from an external account	Payments are to be received from an external account in foreign currency only
4	Credit facilities to non-residents	Non-resident correspondent banks and stock-broking companies were permitted to obtain credit facilities up to RM5 million from domestic banks to fund mismatch of receipts and payments in their external accounts	Domestic credit facilities to non-resident corresponding banks and non-resident stock-broking companies are no longer allowed
5	Investment abroad	Corporate residents with domestic borrowing were allowed to invest abroad up to the equivalent of RM10 million per calendar year on a corporate group basis	Residents with no domestic borrowing are allowed to make payment to non-residents for investment abroad up to an amount of RM10 000 or its equivalent in foreign currency per transaction

6	Credit facilities from non-residents	Residents were allowed to obtain ringgit credit facilities of less than RM100 000 in the aggregate from non-resident individuals	All residents require prior approval to make payments to non-residents for investing abroad an amount exceeding RM100 equivalent in foreign currency. Residents are not allowed to obtain ringgit credit facilities from any non-resident individual
7	Trading in securities	There were no restrictions on secondary trading of securities registered in Malaysia between residents and non-residents and among non-residents For transfer of securities registered outside Malaysia from a non-resident to a resident, the resident was subject to the rules on investment abroad.	Ringgit securities held by non-residents must be transacted through an authorized depositor All payments by non-residents for any security registered in Malaysia must be made from an external account (in foreign currency or in ringgit) All proceeds in ringgit received by a non-resident from the sale of any Malaysian security must be retained in an external account for at least one year before converting to foreign currency All payments to residents for any security registered outside Malaysia from non-residents must be made in foreign currency
8	Import and export of currency notes, bills of exchange, insurance policies etc	A resident or non-resident traveller was free to import or export any amount of ringgit notes or foreign currency notes in person Export of foreign currencies required approval Authorized currency dealers were allowed to import any amount of ringgit notes, subject to reporting to Bank Negara Malaysia on a monthly basis	A resident traveller is permitted to bring in ringgit notes up to RM1000 only and any amount of foreign currencies A resident traveller is permitted to export ringgit notes only up to RM1000 and foreign currencies up to the equivalent of RM10 000. A non-resident traveller is permitted to import ringgit notes up to RM1000 only and any amount of foreign currencies A non-resident traveller is permitted to export ringgit notes up to RM1000 only and foreign currencies up to the amount brought into the country
9	Transaction in the Labuan Offshore Financial Centre	Licensed offshore banks were allowed to trade in ringgit instruments up to permitted limits	Licensed offshore banks are no longer allowed to trade in ringgit instruments

Source: Compiled from Bank Negara Malaysia, *Quarterly Bulletin*, Second Quarter 1998, Kuala Lumpur, and IMF (1997).

Table A.3 Korea: selected economic indicators, 1997Q1–1999Q4[1]

	1996	1997	1998	1999	1997 Q1	1997 Q2	1997 Q3	1997 Q4	1998 Q1	1998 Q2	1998 Q3	1998 Q4	1999 Q1	1999 Q2	1999 Q3	1999 Q4
Growth of GDP (%)	6.8	5.0	–5.8	10.2	6.9	4.9	5.3	1.1	–3.6	–7.2	–7.1	–5.3	4.5	9.9	12.3	—
Growth rate by final demand category (%)																
Private consumption	7.1	3.5	–9.6	—	4.5	4.4	5.3	–0.1	–9.9	–11.2	–10.4	–6.9	6.2	9.1	10.3	—
Public consumption	8.2	1.5	–0.1	—	1.7	2.5	2.3	–0.4	1.3	–0.7	–0.6	–0.4	–1.7	–2.3	–1.3	—
Gross domestic investment	8.3	–7.5	–33.6	—	3.0	–4.8	–11.9	–13.3	–48.7	–43.3	–40.4	–24.2	22.5	30.3	35.1	—
Growth by sector (%)																
Agriculture, forestry and fishing	3.3	4.6	–6.3	—	5.3	4.0	3.8	5.2	6.2	–3.5	–7.0	–9.0	–7.4	5.3	4.2	—
Manufacturing	6.8	6.6	–7.4	21.8	7.1	8.5	6.8	3.4	–4.6	–10.4	–9.1	–4.7	10.3	20.3	26.8	—
Construction	6.9	1.4	–8.6	–10.1	–0.9	2.5	4.8	3.6	–3.9	–6.6	–10.1	–13.3	–14.8	–7.8	–10.0	—
Services	6.2	5.2	–2.2	—	7.8	8.3	7.5	5.1	–1.0	–3.4	–3.0	–1.3	3.3	6.0	7.6	—
Unemployment rate	2.0	2.6	6.8	6.3	—	—	—	—	5.6	6.8	7.4	7.4	8.4	6.6	5.6	4.6
Inflation rate (CPI) (%)	4.9	4.4	7.5	0.8	4.5	4.0	4.2	6.6	8.9	8.2	7.0	6.0	0.7	0.6	0.7	1.3
Growth of money and credit (end of period) %																
M2	15.8	14.1	27.0	28.4	24.7	21.1	23.6	21.1	12.1	16.3	24.8	27.0	33.7	27.1	26.9	28.4
Average bank lending rate (%)	10.0	11.9	15.2	10.8	11.4	11.4	11.6	13.6	17.3	16.9	14.8	11.9	10.6	9.8	11.5	12.2
Growth of real bank credit to the private sector[2]	14.2	13.2	3.8	17.8	17.6	15.8	11.9	14.0	9.0	5.0	5.5	3.8	12.8	15.7	17.0	17.8
Non-performing loans ratio (%)[2,3]	—	—	10.5	—	—	—	—	—	—	—	—	10.5	—	11.3	10.1	—

Average share price index	90.6	67.8	47.1	95.4	69.8	73.9	75.1	61.0	58.3	43.0	36.5	50.6	65.8	90.1	1113.1	112.6
Fiscal deficit as % of GDP	0.03	–0.02	–4.2	—	—	—	—	—	—	—	—	—	—	—	—	—
External transactions																
Merchandise exports (US$, FOB, %)	4.3	5.0	–2.8	9.8	–5.6	7.1	15.6	3.5	8.4	–1.8	–10.8	–5.5	–1.6	2.5	15.2	24.2
Merchandise imports (US$, FOB, %)	12.3	–2.2	–36.1	28.3	3.9	0.8	–3.8	–4.8	–36.2	–37.0	–39.9	–28.7	8.1	22.1	38.6	44.9
Current account balance (as % of GDP)	–4.4	–1.7	12.6	—	–6.3	–2.2	–1.6	3.5	16.1	14.2	11.9	9.1	6.9	6.5	—	—
Foreign reserves (US$ billion)[2]	34.0	20.4	52.0	—	29.9	34.1	30.3	20.3	29.7	40.8	46.9	52.0	57.4	61.9	65.4	—
Total external debt as % of GDP[2]	30.3	33.4	46.4	—	—	—	—	—	—	—	—	46.4	42.3	38.9	36.9	—
Short term foreign debt as % of total debt[2]	—	39.9	20.6	29.0	—	—	—	—	—	—	—	20.6	21.9	22.7	24.8	28.0
Short-term foreign debt as % of foreign reserves[2]		312.3	59.1	50.0	—	—	—	—	—	—	—	59.1	55.5	51.8	53.5	50.0
Average exchange rate (ringgit per US$)	804.5	951.3	1401.4	1188.2	870.3	891.3	908.3	1403.5	1605.7	1394.6	1326.1	1279.3	1196.3	1188.9	1195.0	1172.5

Notes:
1. All growth rates on a year-on-year basis.
2. End of period.
3. Non-performing loans of commercial banks only. Based on a 'six month' non-performing period.

— data not available.

Source: Asian Development Bank, Asia Recovery Information Centre database (*ARIC@adb.org*) and IMF, International Financial Statistics data tapes.

Table A.4 Thailand: selected economic indicators, 1997Q1–1999Q4[1]

					1997				1998				1999			
	1996	1997	1998	1999	Q1	Q2	Q3	Q4	Q1	Q2	Q3	Q4	Q1	Q2	Q3	Q4
Growth of GDP (%)	5.9	–1.8	–10.4	4.0	1.1	–1.6	–2.0	–4.4	–9.0	–12.7	–13.2	–6.6	0.9	3.3	7.7	—
Growth rate by final demand category (%)																
Private consumption	6.8	–0.8	–10.6	—	8.2	3.0	–5.2	–8.6	–10.6	–14.5	–12.8	–3.9	–0.3	1.1	5.5	—
Public consumption	11.9	–3.6	4.0	—	2.2	–3.6	–0.7	–12.1	–6.4	–6.0	–11.9	15.5	1.4	15.5	3.4	—
Gross domestic investment	—	–21.7	–34.8	—	–12.3	–20.8	–21.8	–31.3	–30.6	–59.7	–41.0	–3.3	9.8	13.0	1.8	—
Growth by sector (%)																
Agriculture, forestry and fishing	3.8	–0.6	–1.3	2.9	–1.5	–0.8	–2.5	1.6	–1.2	–3.7	–0.7	2.2	–0.7	3.2	–0.2	—
Manufacturing	6.7	0.1	–11.6	11.1	3.8	5.1	–3.2	–7.5	–13.3	–13.8	–14.8	–4.1	6.6	9.5	17.4	—
Construction	7.2	–26.6	–38.8	–8.5	–31.1	–25.5	–14.3	–36.7	–28.1	–35.8	–41.6	–40.6	–24.8	–18.4	–0.6	—
Services	5.3	–1.1	–9.4	1.4	0.1	–0.2	0.7	1.2	–6.9	–11.9	–11.0	–7.7	–0.4	1.2	3.1	
Unemployment rate	1.1	0.9	4.4	—	—	—	—	—	4.6	5.0	3.4	4.5	5.2	5.3	3.05	—
Inflation rate (CPI) (%)	5.8	5.6	8.1	0.3	4.5	4.4	6.6	7.6	9.0	10.3	8.1	5.0	2.7	0.4	–1.0	0.1
Growth of money and credit (end of period) (%)																
M2	12.6	16.5	9.7	—	11.0	13.2	19.0	16.0	15.7	13.8	12.7	9.7	8.6	5.8	1.9	—
Average bank lending rate (%)	13.4	14.9	14.4	9.4	13.0	12.8	13.9	14.9	15.3	15.3	14.8	12.3	10.3	8.9	8.6	10.0
Growth of real bank credit to the private sector [2]	9.4	13.6	–11.3	—	8.4	5.1	8.4	11.3	3.4	2.5	–5.0	–11.3	–3.6	–4.0	–3.0	—
Non-performing loan (NPL) ratio (%)[2,3]	—	—	45.0	38.5	—	—	—	—	—	32.7	39.7	45.0	47.0	47.4	44.4	38.5

Average share price index	1167.9	597.8	353.9	421.1	754.2	601.4	762.3	443.7	473.1	361.5	246.0	335.0	357.1	461.8	450.5	415.0
Fiscal deficit as % of GDP	1.0	–0.3	–2.8	—	—	—	—	—	—	—	—	—	—	—	—	—
External transactions																
Merchandise exports (US$, FOB, %)	–1.9	4.1	–6.9	7.2	–1.1	2.2	7.1	6.4	–3.4	–5.2	–8.6	–9.9	–3.6	5.7	11.1	16.5
Merchandise imports (US$, FOB, %)	0.6	–13.7	–33.7	17.6	–7.7	–7.6	–1.4	–27.5	–39.8	–38.2	–34.2	–18.9	–1.0	11.7	21.9	38.0
Current account balance (as % of GDP)	–8.1	–2.0	12.7	—	–4.7	–7.1	–1.9	9.6	16.5	10.2	12.5	11.7	10.8	8.6	9.3	—
Foreign reserves (US$ billion)[2]	37.7	26.2	28.8	34.1	37.1	31.4	28.6	26.1	26.9	25.8	26.6	28.8	29.2	30.7	31.6	34.1
Total external debt as % of GDP[2]	49.8	62.0	76.8	—	—	—	—	62.0	70.8	75.1	78.7	76.7	70.4	66.4	66.1	—
Short-term foreign debt as % of total debt[2]	41.5	37.3	27.2	—	—	—	—	37.3	34.2	32.2	30.1	27.2	24.5	21.8	19.9	—
Short-term foreign debt as % of foreign reserves[2]	99.7	133.1	81.4	—	—	—	—	133.1	116.6	110.0	98.2	81.4	70.2	57.2	49.6	—
Average exchange rate (baht per US$)	25.3	31.4	41.4	37.8	25.8	25.6	33.0	40.6	47.1	40.3	41.1	37.0	37.1	37.2	38.4	38.8

Notes:
1. All growth rates on a year-on-year basis.
2. End of period.
3. Non-performing loans of commercial banks only. Based on a 'six month' non-performing period.

— Data not available.

Source: Asian Development Bank, Asia Recovery Information Centre database (*ARIC@adb.org*) and IMF, International Financial Statistics data tapes.

Bibliography

Abidin, Mahani Zainal (2000), 'Malaysia's Alternative Approach to Crisis Management', in Institute of Southeast Asian Studies (ISEAS), *Southeast Asian Affairs 2000*, Singapore: ISEAS, pp. 184–99.

ADB (Asian Development Bank) (1997), *Emerging Asia: Changes and Challenges*, Manila: ADB.

ADB (2000), *Asia Recovery Report 2000*, http://aric.adb.org.

Alavi, Rokiah (1996), *Industrialisation in Malaysia: Import Substitution and Infant Industry Performance*, London: Routledge.

Ariff, Mohamed (1991), *The Malaysian Economy: Pacific Connections*, Kuala Lumpur: Oxford University Press.

Ariff, Mohamed (1999), 'The Financial Crisis and the Reshaping of the Malaysian Economy: Trends and Issues', unpublished paper, Malaysian Institute of Economic Research, Kuala Lumpur.

Athukorala, Prema-chandra (1997), 'Malaysia', in Asia Pacific Study Group, *Asia Pacific Economic Profiles 1997*, Hong Kong: Financial Times Newsletters and Management Reports, pp. 203–31.

Athukorala, Prema-chandra (1998a), *Trade Policy Issues in Asian Development*, London: Routledge.

Athukorala, Prema-chandra (1998b), 'Malaysia', in Ross H. McLeod and Ross Garnaut (eds), *East Asia in Crisis: from being a Miracle to Needing One?*, London: Routledge, pp. 85–101.

Athukorala, Prema-chandra (1999), 'Swimming Against the Tide: Crisis management in Malaysia', *ASEAN Economic Bulletin*, 15: 281–9.

Athukorala, Prema-chandra (2000a), 'The Malaysian Experiment', in Peter Drysdale (ed.), *Reforms and Recovery in East Asia: The Role of the State and Economic Enterprise*, London: Routledge, pp. 170–90.

Athukorala, Prema-chandra (2000b), 'Capital Mobility, Crisis and Adjustment: A Malaysian Case Study', *ICSEAD Discussion Paper No. 2000–16*, International Centre for the Study of East Asian Development, Kitakyushu (Japan).

Athukorala, Prema-chandra (2001), 'Malaysia: The Macroeconomy,' in C. Barlow (ed.), *Modern Malaysia in the Global Economy: Political and Social Changes into the 21st Century*, Aldershot: Edward Elgar (forthcoming).

Athukorala, Prema-chandra and Hal Hill (2000), 'FDI and Host Country Development: The East Asian Experience', *Trade and Development Working Paper No. 00/08*, Division of Economics, Research School of Pacific and Asian Studies, Australian National University, Canberra. (Forthcoming in Bijit Bora (ed.), *Research Issues in FDI*, London, Routledge.)

Athukorala, Prema-chandra and Chris Manning (1999), *Structural Adjustment and International Labour Migration in East Asia: Adjusting to Labour Scarcity*, Melbourne: Oxford University Press.

Athukorala, Prema-chandra and Jayant Menon (1995a), 'Developing with Foreign Investment: Malaysia', *Australian Economic Review*, 1st quarter, 9–22.

Athukorala, Prema-chandra and Jayant Menon (1995b), 'Export-led Industrialisation, Employment and Equity: The Malaysian Case', *Agenda*, 4(1), 63–76.

Athukorala, Prema-chandra and Jayant Menan (1999), 'Outward Orientation and Economic Performance: The Malaysian Experience', *World Economy*, *22*(8), 1119–39.

Athukorala, Prema-chandra and Peter Warr (1999), 'Vulnerability to a Currency Crisis: lessons from the Asian Experience', *Working Papers in Trade and Development No. 99/6*, Division of Economics, Research School of Pacific and Asian Studies, Asia Pacific School of Economics and Management, Australian National University.

Bäckström, Urban (1997), 'What lessons can be learned from recent financial crises? The Swedish experience', in Federal Reserve Bank of Kansas City, *Maintaining Financial Stability in a Global Economy*, Jackson Hole, Wyoming: Federal Reserve Bank of Kansas City, pp. 55–96.

Bank Negara Malaysia (various, from 1995), *Monthly Statistical Bulletin*, Kuala Lumpur.

Barro, Robert J. (1998), 'Malaysia could do Worse than this Economic Plan', *Business Week*, 2 November, p. 11.

Bertrand, Raymond (1981), 'The Liberalisation of Capital Movements – An Insight', *The Three Bank Review*, 132, December.

Bhagwati, Jagdish (1998a), 'The Capital Myth: The Difference between Trade in Widgets and Dollars', *Foreign Affairs*, 77(3), 7–12.

Bhagwati, Jagdish (1998b), 'Asian Financial Crisis Debate: Why? How Severe?', paper presented at the conference on *Managing the Asian Financial Crisis*: *Lessons and Changes*, organized by the Asian Strategic Leadership Institute and Rating Agency Malaysia, 2 and 3 November, Kuala Lumpur.

BIS (Bank for International Settlements) (1998), *International Banking and Financial Market Development*, Basle: BIS.

BNM (Bank Negara Malaysia) (1994), *Money and Banking in Malaysia*, Kuala Lumpur: BNM.

BNM (Bank Negara Malaysia) (1999a), *Annual Report of the Board of Directors for the Year Ended 31 December 1998*, Kuala Lumpur: BNM.

BNM (Bank Negara Malaysia) (1999b), *The Central Bank and the Financial System in Malaysia*, Kuala Lumpur: BNM.

BNM (Bank Negara Malaysia) (2000a), *Quarterly Review – 4th Quarter 1999*, Kuala Lumpur: BNM (*http://www.bnm.gov.my*).

BNM (Bank Negara Malaysia) (2000b), *The 1999 Annual Survey on Manufacturing Companies*, Kuala Lumpur: BNM.

Booth, Anne (1999), 'Initial Conditions and Miraculous Growth: Why is Southeast Asia Different from Taiwan and South Korea?', *World Development*, 27(2), 301–21.

Branson, William H. (1993), 'A Comment on John Williamson's Paper', in Melmut Reisen and Bernhard Fischer (eds), *Financial Opening: Policy Issues and Experiences in Developing Countries*, Paris: OECD, pp. 35–7.

Bruton, Henry J. (1993), *The Political Economy of Poverty, Equity and Growth: Sri Lanka and Malaysia*, New York: Oxford University Press.

Calvo, Guillermo A. (1995), 'Varieties of Capital-Market Crises', *Center for International Economics Working Paper* No. 15, College Park: University of Maryland.

Calvo, Guillermo and Enrique Medoza (1996), 'Petty Crime and Cruel Punishment: Lessons from the Mexican Debacle', *American Economic Review*, 86 (May), 170–75.

Calvo, Guillermo, Leonardo Leiderman and Carmen Reinhart (1995), 'Capital Inflows to Latin America with Reference to Asian Experience', in Sebastian Edwards (ed.), *Capital Controls, Exchange Rates and Monetary Policy in the World Economy*, Cambridge: Cambridge University Press.

Cardenas, Mauricio and Felpe Barrera (1998), 'On the Effectiveness of Capital Controls: The Experience of Colombia During the 1990s', *Journal of Development Economics*, 54: 27–57.

Chang, Ha-Joon, Hong-Jae Park and Chul Gye You (1998), 'Interpreting the Korean crisis', *Cambridge Journal of Economics*, 22: 735–46.

Claessens, Stijn, Simon Djankov and Larry H.P. Lang (1999a), 'Who controls East Asian Companies?', *Policy Research Working Paper 2054*, World Bank.

Claessens, Stijn, Simon Djankov and Larry H.P. Lang (1999b), 'Looking at Corporate Asia', in Alison Harwood, Robert E. Litan and Michael Pomerleano (eds), *Financial Markets and Development: The Crisis in Emerging Markets*, Washington, DC: Brookings Institution Press, pp. 159–78.

Cooper, Richard N. (1996), 'Comments on Sachs, Tornell and Velasco', *Brookings Papers on Economic Activity*, 1: 203–8.

Cooper, Richard N. (1998), 'Comments on the paper by Radelet and Sachs', *Brookings Papers on Economic Activity*, 2: 90–92.

Cooper, Richard N. (1999a), 'The Asian Crises: Causes and Consequences', in Alison Harwood, Robert E. Litan and Michael Pomerleano (eds), *Financial Markets and Development: The Crisis in Emerging Markets*, Washington, DC: Brookings Institution Press, pp. 17–28.

Cooper, Richard N. (1999b), 'Should capital controls be banished?', *Brookings Papers on Economic Activity*, 1: 89–125.

Cooper, Richard N. and Jeffrey Sachs (1985), 'Borrowing Abroad: the Debtor's Perspective', in Gorden W. Smith and John T. Cuddington (eds), *International Debt and Developing Countries*, Washington, DC: World Bank, pp. 21–60.

Corbett, Jenny and David Vines (1999), 'The Asian Crises: Lessons from Vulnerability, Crisis and Collapse', *World Economy*, 22(2), 155–77.

Corbo, Vittorio and Jaime de Melo (1987), 'Lessons from the Southern Cone Policy Reforms', *World Bank Research Observer*, 2(1), 111–42.

Corden, W. Max (1996), *Pragmatic Orthodoxy: Macroeconomic Policies in Seven East Asian Economies*, San Francisco: International Center for Economic Growth.

Corden, W. Max (1998), 'Sense and Nonsense on the Asian Crisis', The Sturc Lecture, 5 November, Paul H. Nitze School of Advanced International Studies, Johns Hopkins University, Washington, DC.

Corden, W. Max (1999), *The Asian Crisis: Is There a Way Out*?, Singapore: Institute of Southeast Asian Studies.

Corsetti, Giancarlo, Paolo Pesenti and Nouriel Roubini (1998), 'What caused the Asian Currency and Financial Crisis?', paper presented at the CEPR/World Bank conference, *Financial Crises: Contagion and Market Volatility*, 8–9 May, London.

Cowan, Kevin and Jose de Gregorio (1998), 'Exchange Rate Policies and Capital Account Management', in Reuven Glick (ed.), *Managing Capital Flows and Exchange Rates: Perspectives for the Pacific Basin*, Cambridge: Cambridge University Press.

Crotty, James R. (1983), 'On Keynes and Capital Flight', *Journal of Economic Literature*, 21(1), 59–65.

Crouch, Harold (1994), 'Industrialisation and Political Change', in Harold Brookfield (ed.), *Transformation with Industrialisation in Peninsular Malaysia*, Kuala Lumpur: Oxford University Press, pp. 14–34.

Crouch, Harold (1996), *Government & Society in Malaysia*, Sydney: Allen & Unwin.

Crouch, Harold (1998), 'The Asian Economic Crisis and Democracy', *Public Policy*, 11(3), 39–62.

Danaharta (National Asset Management Company, Malaysia) (1999), *Operations Report, 20 June–21 December 1998*, Kuala Lumpur.

De Gregorio, Jose, Sebastian Edwards and Rodrigo O. Valdes (1998), 'Capital Controls in Chile: An Assessment', paper for the 1998 IASE-NBER Conference, Center for Applied Economics, Department of Industrial Engineering, Universidad de Chile, Santiago (photocopy).

DeLong, J. Bradford (1999), 'Financial Crises in the 1980s and the 1990s: Must History Repeat?', *Brookings Papers on Economic Activity*, 2: 253–94.

Diaz-Alejandro, Carlos F. (1965), *Exchange Rate Devaluation in a Semi-Industrialized Economy: The Experience of Argentina, 1955–1961*, Cambridge, Mass.: MIT Press.

Diaz-Alejandro, Carlos F. (1985), 'Good-bye Financial Repression, Hello Financial Crash', *Journal of Development Economics*, 19(1), 1–24.

Dooley, Michael P. (1995), 'A Survey of Academic Literature on Controls over International Capital Transactions', *NBER Working Paper 5352*, Cambridge, Mass.: National Bureau of Economic Research.

Dooley, Michael (2000), 'A Model of Crises in Emerging Markets', *Economic Journal*, 110: 256–72.

Dornbusch, Rudiger (1993), *Stabilization, Debt and Reforms: Policy Analysis for Developing Countries*, Englewood Cliffs, NJ: Prentice-Hall.

Dornbusch, Rudiger (1997), 'A Thai–Mexico primer: Lessons for outmaneuvering a financial meltdown', *The International Economy*, September/October, 20–23 & 55.

Dornbusch, Rudiger and Sebastian Edwards (1994), 'Trade and Exchange Rate Policies', in Barry P. Bosworth, Rudiger Dornbusch and Raul Laban (eds), *The Chilean Economy: Policy Lessons and Challenges*, Washington, DC: Brookings Institution.

Dornbusch, Rudiger and Yung Chul Park (eds) (1995), *Financial Opening*, San Francisco: International Center for Economic Growth.

Dornbusch, Rudiger, Iian Goldfajn and Rodrigo O. Valdes (1995), 'Currency crises and collapses', *Brookings Papers on Economic Activity*, 2: 219–93.

Economic Strategy Institute (1999), *State of Asia*, Washington, DC: Economic Strategy Institute.

The Economist (1997a), 'Murky Corporate Governance', 20 December, p. 111.

The Economist (1997b), 'Mahathir, Soros and the Currency Market', 27 September, p.93.

The Economist (1999), 'The Road less Travelled', 1 May, p.79.

The Economist (2000), 'Straggles', 5 August, pp. 74–5.

Edgardo, Jose E. and Hilton L. Root (1996), *The Key to the Asian Miracle: Making Shared Growth Credible*, Washington, DC: Brookings Institution.

Edwards, Sebastian (1984), 'The Order of Liberalization of the External

Sector in Developing Countries', *Princeton Essays in International Finance 156*, Princeton University.

Edwards, Sebastian (1989), *Real Exchange Rates, Devaluation and Adjustment: Exchange Rate Policies in Developing Countries*, Cambridge, Mass: MIT Press.

Edwards, Sebastian (1998), 'Asia Should Beware of Chilean-style Capital Controls', *Asian Wall Street Journal*, 8 September.

Edwards, Sebastian (1999a), 'A Capital Idea? Reconsidering a Financial Quick Fix', *Foreign Affairs*, 78(3), 18–22.

Edwards, Sebastian (1999b), 'On Crisis Prevention: Lessons from Mexico and East Asia', in Alison Harwood, Robert E. Litan and Michael Pomerleano (eds), *Financial Markets and Development: The Crisis in Emerging Markets*, Washington, DC: Brookings Institution Press, pp. 269–334.

Edwards, Sebastian and Moshin Khan (1985), 'Interest Rate Determination in Developing Countries; A Conceptual Framework', *IMF Staff Papers*, 32: 377–403.

Eichengreen, Barry (1998), *Globalizing Capital: A History of the International Monetary System*, Princeton, NJ: Princeton University Press.

Eichengreen, Barry (1999), *Toward a New International Financial Architecture: A Practical Post-Asia Agenda*, Washington, DC: Institute for International Economics.

Eichengreen, Barry and Michael Mussa (1998), 'Capital Account Liberalization: Theoretical and Practical Aspects', *IMF Occasional Paper 172*, Washington, DC: IMF.

Eichengreen, Barry and Jeffrey Sachs (1985), 'Exchange Rate and Economic Recovery in the 1930s', *Journal of Economic History*, 45(4), 925–46.

EIU (Economist Intelligence Unit) (1998), *Country Economic Report: Malaysia and Brunei*, 3rd Quarter, London: EIU.

EPU (Economic Planning Unit, Malaysia) (1999), *Status of the Malaysian Economy* (*http://epu.jpm.my/white*).

Federal Reserve Bank of Kansas City (1997), *Maintaining Financial Stability in a Global Economy: A Symposium*, Kansas City: Federal Reserve Bank of Kansas City (also available at the Bank's web site: *http://www.ke.frb.org*).

FEER (*Far Eastern Economic Review*) (1997a), 'Thus Spake Mahathir', 18 September, p. 65.

FEER (*Far Eastern Economic Review*) (1997b), 'Malaysia: Hit the Brake', 18 December, pp. 14–15.

FEER (*Far Eastern Economic Review*) (1998), 'Free Thinker' (interview with Jagdish Bhagwati), 15 October, p. 14.

FEER (*Far Eastern Economic Review*) (1999), 'Politically Incorrect' (interview with Lee Kuan Yew), 24 September, pp. 11–12.

Feldstein, Martin (1995), 'Global Capital Flows: Too Little, not too Much', *The Economist*, 24 June, pp. 76–8.

Feldstein, Matin (1998), 'Refocussing the IMF', *Foreign Affairs*, 77: 20–33.

Felker, Greg (2000), 'Malaysia in 1999: Mahathir's Pyrrhic Deliverance', *Asian Survey*, 40(1), 49–60.

Financial Times (1998), 'Asia in Crisis' (5 Part Series), 12–16 January.

Fischer, Stanley (1998), 'Lessons from a crisis', *The Economist*, 3 October, pp. 19–23.

Fischer, Stanley (1999), 'The Road to Sustainable Recovery in Asia', Washington, DC: IMF (*http://www.imf.org/external/np/speeches/1999/101899*).

Fisher, Irvin (1933), 'The Debt–Deflation Theory of Great Depression', *Econometrica*, 1: 337–57.

Folkerts-Landau, David (1999), 'The Development Prospects and Regulation', in Alison Harwood, Robert E. Litan and Michael Pomerleano (eds), *Financial Markets and Development: The Crisis in Emerging Markets*, Washington, DC: Brookings Institution Press, pp. 404–8.

FPB (*Foreign Policy Bulletin*) (1997), 'SE Asia Currency Crisis Focus of IMF/World Bank Annual Meeting' (Excerpts from Statements by Malaysian Prime Minister Mahathir Mohamad, George Soros and Michel Camdessus), *FPB*, 8(6), 24–33.

Furman, Jason and Joseph Stiglitz (1998), 'Economic Crises: Evidence and Insights from East Asia', *Brookings Papers on Economic Activity*, 2: 1–136.

Gan, Wee Beng and Lee Ying Soon (1998), 'Input Versus Productivity Driven Growth: Implications for the Malaysian Growth', in Lee Ying Soon and Shyamala Nagajaj (eds), *The Seventh Malaysia Plan: Productivity for Sustainable Development*, Kuala Lumpur: University of Malaya Press, pp. 39–58.

Garnaut, Ross (1998), 'The Financial Crisis: A Watershed in Economic Thought about East Asia', *Asian Pacific Economic Literature*, 12: 1–11.

Gavin, Michael, Ricardo Hausmann and Leonardo Leiderman (1996), 'The Macroeconomics of Capital Flows to Latin America: Experience and Policy Issues', in Ricardo Hausmann and Liliana Rojas-Suarez (eds), *Volatile Capital Flows: Taming Their Impact on Latin America*, Washington, DC: Inter-American Development Bank, pp. 1–40.

Goad, Pierre (1999), 'Optimism vs. Medicine', *Far Eastern Economic Review*, 17 June, p. 38.

Goldstein, Morris (1998), *The Asian Financial Crisis: Causes, Cures and Systemic Implications*, Washington, DC: Institute for International Economics.

Goldstein, Morris and Carmen Reinhart (1998), *Forecasting Financial Cri-*

ses: Early Warning Signals for Emerging Markets, Washington, DC: Institute for International Economics.

Gomez, Edmund T. and K.S. Jomo (1997), *Malaysia's Political Economy: Politics, Patronage and Profits*, Cambridge: Cambridge University Press.

Government of Malaysia (1996), *Seventh Malaysia Plan 1996–2000*, Kuala Lumpur: National Printing Department.

Government of Malaysia (1998), *The 1999 Budget Speech*, 23 October, Kuala Lumpur: Ministry of Finance.

Government of Malaysia (1999), *Economic Survey – 1999*, Kuala Lumpur: Ministry of Finance.

Granwille, Steven A. (1998), 'The Asian Economic Crisis', *Reserve Bank of Australia Bulletin*, April, 9–20.

Hale, David (1997), 'Rubin's Folly?', *The International Economy*, September/October, 14–19.

Hale, David (1998), 'The Hot Money Debate', *The International Economy*, November/December, 8–12 & 66–9.

Hall, Thomas E. and J. David Ferguson (1998), *The Great Depression: An International Disaster of Perverse Economic Policies*, Ann Arbor: University of Michigan Press.

Harvey, Campbell R. and Andrew H. Roper (1999), 'The Asian Bet', in Alison Hardwood, Robert E. Litan and Michael Pomerleano (eds), *Financial Markets and Development: The Crisis in Emerging Markets*, Washington, DC: Brookings Institution Press, pp.29–116.

Helleiner, Gerald K. (1998), 'Capital Account Regimes and the Developing Countries: Issues and Approaches', in Gerald K. Helleiner (ed.), *Capital Account Regimes and the Developing Countries*, London: Macmillan, pp.1–44.

Henderson, Callum (1998), *Asia Falling? Making Sense of the Asian Currency Crisis and its Aftermath*, Singapore: McGraw-Hill.

Hiebert, Murray (1998), 'Big Isn't Beautiful', *Far Eastern Economic Review*, 5 March, pp. 44–6.

Hiebert, Murray (1999), 'Capital Idea?', *Far Eastern Economic Review*, 1 July, 55.

Hiebert, Murray and S. Jayasankaran (1999), 'Malaysia: Wake-up Call', *Far Eastern Economic Review*, 18 March, 18–11.

Hill, Hal (1998), 'Malaysian Roulette', *Asian Wall Street Journal*, 9–10 October.

Holloway, Nigel (1997), 'All Together Now: Needed Banking Standards for a Volatile Region', *Far Eastern Economic Review*, 22 May, 83–4.

Hong, Wontack (1990), 'Export-Oriented Growth of Korea: A Possible Path to Advanced Economy', *International Economic Journal*, 4(2), 1–24.

Huhne, Christopher (1998), 'How the rating agencies blew it on Korea: An industry insider's honest admission', *The International Economy*, May/June, 46–9.

Husted, Steven and Ronald MacDonald (1999), 'The Asian Currency Crash: Were Badly Driven Fundamentals to Blame?', *Journal of Asian Economics*, 1(4), 537–50.

IMF (International Monetary Fund) (1997), *Exchange Arrangements and Exchange Restrictions, Annual Report 1997*, Washington, DC: IMF.

IMF (1999), 'Public Information Notice No. 99/88: IMF Concludes Article IV Consultation with Malaysia, Washington, DC: IMF (*www.imf.org/external/np/sec/pn/1999/pn9988.htm*).

IMF (1999b), *International Capital Markets: Developments, Prospects and Key Policy Issues*, Washington, DC: IMF.

IMF (1999c), 'Symposium "Getting it Right: Sequencing of Financial Sector Reforms"', 15 June (transcript) (*www.imf.org/external/np/tr/1999/tr990715.htm*).

IMF (2000), 'Public Information Notice No. 00/63: IMF Concludes Article IV Consultation with Malaysia, Washington, DC: IMF (*www.imf.org/external/np/sec/pn/2000/pn0063.htm*).

Ito, Takatoshi (1999), 'Capital Flows in Asia', *NBER Working Paper 7134*, Cambridge, Mass: NBER.

Jayasankaran, S. and Nate Thayer (1996), 'Investment: From Logs to Lotus', *Far Eastern Economic Review*, 12 December, 64–8.

Jesudason, James (1989), *Ethnicity and the Economy: The State, Chinese Business and Multinationals in Malaysia*, Singapore: Oxford University Press.

Johnson, Bryan T. and Thomas P. Sheehy (1995), *The Index of Economic Freedom*, Washington, DC: Heritage Foundation.

Jomo, K.S. (1998), 'Malaysian Debacle: Whose Fault?', *Cambridge Journal of Economics*, 27(4), 707–22.

Jomo, K.S. and Associates (1997), *Southeast Asia's Misunderstood Miracle: Industrial Policy and Economic Development in Thailand, Malaysia and Indonesia*, Boulder, Col.: Westview Press.

Kaminsky, Graciela, Saul Lizondo and Carmen M. Reinhart (1997), 'Leading indicators of currency crises', *IMF Working Paper WP/97/79*, Washington, DC: IMF.

Kassim, Azizah (2000), 'Country report: Malaysia', paper presented at the Japan Institute Labour Workshop on *International Migration and Labour in Asia*, Tokyo, 26–8 January.

Keynes, John Maynard (1925), 'The Economic Consequences of Mr. Churchill', reproduced in J.M. Keynes (1963), *Essays in Persuasion*, New York: W.W. Norton, pp. 244–70.

Kim, Sunho (2000), 'Capital Market Liberalisation', in Heather Smith (ed.), *Looking Forward: Korea after the Economic Crisis*, Canberra: Asia Pacific Press at the Australian National University, pp. 105–26.

Kindleberger, Charles P. (1986), *The World in Depression, 1929–1939*, Harmondsworth: Penguin.

Kindleberger, Charles P. (1996), *Manias, Panics and Crashes: A History of Financial Crises*, 3rd edn, New York: John Wiley & Sons.

Kraay, Aart (1998), 'Do High Interest Rates Defend Currencies During Speculative Attacks?, mimeo, World Bank, Washington, DC.

Kregal, J.A. (1998), 'East Asia is not Mexico: The Difference between Balance of Payments Crises and Debt Deflation', in K.S. Jomo (ed.), *Tigers in Trouble: Financial Governance, Liberalisation, and Crisis in East Asia*, London: Zed Books Ltd., 44–62.

Krueger, Anne O. (1984), 'Problems of Liberalization', in Arnold C. Harberger (ed.), *World Economic Growth*, San Francisco, Cal.: ICS Press.

Krueger, Anne O. (1992), *Economic Policy Reforms in Developing Countries*, Oxford: Basil Blackwell.

Krueger, Anne O. and Aron Tornell (1999), 'The Role of Bank Restructuring in Recovering from Crisis', *NBER Working Paper No. 7042*, Cambridge, Mass.: National Bureau of Economic Research.

Krugman, Paul (1979), 'A Model of Balance of Payments Crises', *Journal of Money Credit and Banking*, 11(3), 311–25.

Krugman, Paul (1991),'International aspects of financial crises', in Martin Feldstein (ed.), *The Risk of Economic Crisis*, Chicago: University of Chicago Press, pp. 85–109.

Krugman, Paul (1994), 'The Myth of Asia's Miracle', *Foreign Affairs*, 73(1), 62–78.

Krugman, Paul (1995), 'Growing World Trade: Causes and Consequences', *Brooking Papers on Economic Activity*, 25th Anniversary Issue, 327–77.

Krugman, Paul (1996), 'Are Currency Crises Self-Fulfilling?', in *NBER Macroeconomic Annual 1996*, Cambridge, Mass.: MIT Press, pp. 311–28.

Krugman, Paul (1997), 'Latin Lessons for Asia', *Far Eastern Economic Review*, 25 September, p. 35.

Krugman, Paul (1998a), 'Malaysia's Opportunity', *Far Eastern Economic Review*, 17 September, p. 17.

Krugman, Paul (1998b), 'Saving Asia: It's Time to get Radical', *Fortune*, 138(5), 74–80.

Krugman, Paul (1998c), 'Fire-sale FDI', *http://web.mit.edu/krugman/www*.

Krugman, Paul (1999a), 'What Happened to Asia?', in Ryuzo Sato, Rama Ramachandran and Kazuo Mino (eds), *Global Competition and Integration*, Boston: Kluwer Academic Publishers, pp. 315–28.

Krugman, Paul (1999b), *The Return of Depression Economics*, New York: Norton and Company.

Krugman, Paul (1999c), 'Capital Control Freaks', *Slate Online Magazine* (*http://slate.msn.com/99-09-27/dismal*).

Krugman, Paul (1999d), 'Recovery? Don't Bet on it', *Time* (Asia edition), 21 June.

Lee, Eddy (1998), *The Asian Financial Crisis: The Challenges for Social Policy*, Geneva: International Labour Organisation.

Leigh, Michael (1992), 'Politics, Bureaucracy, and Business in Malaysia: Realigning the Eternal Triangle', in Andrew J. MacIntyre and Kanishka Jayasuriya (eds), *The Dynamics of Economic Policy Reforms in South-east Asia and the South-west Pacific*, Singapore: Oxford University Press, pp. 115–37.

Lim, David (1992), 'The Dynamics of Economic Policy-making: A Study of Malaysian Trade Policies and Performance', in Andrew J. MacIntyre and Kanishka Jayasuriya (eds), *The Dynamics of Economic Policy Reforms in South-east Asia and the South-west Pacific*, Singapore: Oxford University Press, pp. 94–114.

Lim, Linda (1999), 'Malaysia's Response to the Asian Financial Crisis', statement before the Subcommittee on Asia and the Pacific Committee on International Relations, US House of Representatives, *<http://www.house.gov/international_relations*.

Lucas, Robert E.B. and Donald Verry (1999), *Restructuring the Malaysian Economy: Development and Human Resources*, London: Macmillan.

Macfarlane, Ian J. (1997), 'The Changing Nature of Economic Crises', *Reserve Bank of Australia Bulletin*, December, 17–22.

Mahathir, Dato' Seri Bin Mohamad (1998), *Currency Turmoil: Selected Speeches and Articles by Prime Minister of Malaysia*, Kuala Lumpur: Limkokwing Integrated.

Mahathir, Dato' Seri Bin Mohamad (1999a), *A New Deal for Asia*, Kuala Lumpur: Pelanduk Publications.

Mahathir, Dato' Seri Bin Mohamad (1999b), 'Why Malaysia's Selective Currency Controls are Necessary and Why They Have Worked', paper presented at the *Symposium of the First Anniversary of Currency Control*, 2 October 1999, Nikko Hotel, Kuala Lumpur.

Massad, Carlos (1998), 'The Liberalization of the Capital Account: Chile in the 1990s', in *Princeton Essays in International Finance* (special issue on *Should the IMF Pursue Capital Account Liberalization?*), Princeton, NJ: International Finance Section, Princeton University.

Mazumdar, Dipak (1981), *The Urban Labour Market and Income Distribution: A Study of Malaysia*, New York: Oxford University Press.

McCarthy, Terry (1998), 'It is Dr. Mahathir's Economy Now', *Time*, 5 October, pp. 54–5.

McKinnon, Ronald I. (1998), 'Exchange Rate Coordination for Surmounting the East Asian Crisis', *Asian Economic Journal*, 12: 317–29.

McKinnon, Ronald R. (1991), *The Order of Economic Liberalization: Financial Control in the Transition to a Market Economy*, Baltimore: Johns Hopkins University.

Meade, James (1951), *The theory of International Economic Policy, Volume 1: The Balance of Payments*, London: Oxford University Press, ch. XXII.

Merrill Lynch & Company (1999), *Malaysia: Relaxation of Capital Controls*, February, Kuala Lumpur: Merrill Lynch & Company.

Michaely, Michael, D. Papageorgiou and Armine M. Choksi (1991), *Liberalizing Foreign Trade: Lessons of Experience in the Developing World*, Oxford: Basil Blackwell.

MIER (Malaysian Institute of Economic Research) (1999), *The Impact of Currency Control Measures on Business Operation*, Kuala Lumpur: MIER.

Miller, Merton (1998), 'Asian financial crisis', *Japan and the World Economy*, 10: 355–8.

Miller, Merton H. (1999), 'Reflections of a Retiring Keynote Speaker', keynote address at the 10th Annual Conference of PACAP/FMA, Singapore, July.

Mishkin, Frederic S. (1996), 'Understanding Financial Crises: A Developing Country Perspective', *Annual World Bank Conference on Development Economics*, pp. 29–61.

Mishkin, Frederic S. (1997), 'The Causes and Propagation of Financial Instability: Lessons for Policy Makers' in Federal Reserve Bank of Kansas City, *Maintaining Financial Stability in a Global Economy*, Jackson Hole, Wyoming, Federal Reserve Bank of Kansas City, pp. 55–96.

Mundell, Robert (1968), *International Economics*, New York: Macmillan.

Narayanan, Suresh (1996), 'Fiscal reform in Malaysia: Behind a Successful Experience', *Asian Survey*, 36(9), 869–81.

Narayanan, Suresh (1998), 'Towards Economic Recovery: The Fiscal Policy Side', paper presented at the *1998 National Outlook Conference*, Malaysian Institute of Economic Research, 1–2 December, Kuala Lumpur

Naughton, Barry (1996), 'China's emergence and prospects as a trading nation', *Brookings Papers on Economic Activity*, 2: 293–344.

NEAC (National Economic Action Council) (1998), *National Economic Recovery Plan: Agenda for Action*, Kuala Lumpur: Prime Minister's Department.

NEAC (National Economic Action Council) (1999), 'Prof. Merton is Wrong', Kuala Lumpur, <*http://neac.gov.my*>.

Nellor, David (2000), 'Searching for a New Exchange Rate Regime for Asia', paper presented at the *Financial Markets and Policies in East Asia* conference, 4–5 September, Australian National University, Canberra.

Nidhiprabha, Bhanupong (1999), 'Economic crises and the debt deflation episode in Thailand', *ASEAN Economic Bulletin*, 15: 309–18.

Nidhiprabha, Bhanupong and Peter Warr (2000), 'Thailand's Experience with the Reforms in the Financial Sector', in Peter Drysdale (ed.), *Reforms and Recovery in East Asia: The Role of the State and Economic Enterprise*, London: Routledge, pp. 99–119.

Obstfeld, Maurice (1996), 'Models of Currency Crises with Self-fulfilling Features', *European Economic Review*, 45(1), 61–77.

Obsfeld, Maurice (1998), 'The Global Capital Market: Benefactor or Menace?', *National Bureau of Economic Research Working Paper No. 6559*, Boston, Mass: NBER.

Ogus, Simon (2000), 'Malaysian Twilight Zone', *The International Economy*, May/June, 44–7.

Pillai, Patrick (1995), 'Malaysia', Special Issue on Labour Migration in Asia, *Asean Economic Bulletin*, 12(2), 221–36.

Pomerleano, Michael (1998), 'The East Asian Crisis and Corporate Finances: The Untold Microeconomic Story', *Emerging Markets Quarterly*, 2 (Winter), 14–27.

Pomerleano, Michael and Xin Zhang (1999), 'Corporate Fundamentals and the Behaviour of Capital Markets in Asia', in Alison Harwood, Robert E. Litan and Michael Pomerleano (eds), *Financial Markets and Development: The Crisis in Emerging Markets*, Washington, DC: Brookings Institution Press, pp. 117–57

Radelet, Steve and Jeffrey Sachs (1997), 'Asia's Reemergence', *Foreign Affairs*, 76(6), 44–59.

Radelet, Steve and Jeffrey Sachs (1998), 'The East Asian financial crisis: Diagnosis, remedies, prospects', *Brookings Papers on Economic Activity*, 2: 1–89.

Rahman, Matiur (1998), 'The Role of Accounting Disclosure in the East Asian Financial Crisis: Lessons learned?', UNCTAD, Geneva (mimeo).

Rajan, Ramakishen S. (2000), '[Ir]relevance of Currency Crisis Theory to the Devaluation and Collapse of the Thai Baht', *CIES Policy Discussion Paper 0030*, Centre of International Economic Studies, University of Adelaide (forthcoming in *Princeton Essays in International Finance*).

Rashid, Rehman (1997), *A Malaysian Journey*, Kuala Lumpur: Academe Art & Printing Service.

Reisen, Helmut (1993), 'Southeast Asia and the "Impossible Trinity"', *International Economic Insights*, 4(3) (May/June), 21–3.

Rodrik, Dani (1998), 'Who Needs Capital Account Capital Account Convertibility?', in *Princeton Essays in International Finance 207* (special issue on *Should the IMF Pursue Capital Account Liberalization?*), Princeton, NJ: International Finance Section, Princeton University.

Rodrik, Dani (1999), *The New Global Economy and Developing Countries: Making Openness Work*, Washington, DC: Overseas Development Council (distributed by Johns Hopkins University Press).

Rogoff, Kenneth (1999), 'International Institutions for Reducing Global Financial Instability', *National Bureau of Economic Research Working Paper No. 7265*, Boston, Mass.: NBER.

Sachs, Jeffrey D. (1985), 'External Debt and Macroeconomic Performance in Latin America and East Asia', *Brookings Papers on Economic Activity*, 2: 523–73.

Sachs, Jeffrey D. (1998), 'Glimmers of Hope', *Far Eastern Economic Review*, 5 November, p. 53.

Sachs, Jeffrey D. and Andrew Warner (1995), 'Economic Reforms and the Process of Global Integration', *Brookings Papers on Economic Activity*, 25th Anniversary Issue, 1–95.

Sachs, Jeffrey D., Aaron Tornell and Andrew Velasco (1996), 'Financial crises in emerging markets: The lessons from 1995', *Brookings Papers on Economic Activity*, 1: 147–215.

Salleh, Ismail Muhd and Saha Dhevan Meyanathan (1993), *Malaysia: Growth, Equity and Structural Transformation*, Washington, DC: World Bank.

Scott, Kenneth E. (1999), 'Corporate Governance and East Asia: Korea, Indonesia, Malaysia and Thailand', in Alison Harwood, Robert E. Litan and Michael Pomerleano (eds), *Financial Markets and Development: The Crisis in Emerging Markets*, Washington, DC: Brookings Institution Press, pp. 335–65.

Searle, Peter (1999), *The Riddle of Malaysian Capitalism: Rent-seekers or Real Capitalists?*, Sydney: Allen & Unwin.

Siamwalla, Ammar (2000), 'Anatomy of the Thai Economic Crisis', Thailand Development Research Institute, Bangkok (unpublished manuscript).

Smogyi, Jamos (1991), 'Malaysia's Successful Reform Experience', *Finance and Development*, March, 34–6.

Snodgrass, Donald R. (1980), *Inequality and Economic Development in Malaysia*, Kuala Lumpur: Oxford University Press.

Snodgrass, Donald R. (1993), 'Malaysia: The Next NIC?', *International Economic Insights*, 4(3), 8–11.

Snodgrass, Donald R. (1995), 'Successful Economic Development in a Multiethnic Society: The Malaysian Case', Development Discussion Paper No. 503, Harvard Institute for International Development, Harvard University.

Soros, George (1998), *The Crisis of Global Capitalism*, London: Little, Brown and Company.

Stiglitz, Joseph (1998), 'More Instruments and Broader Goals: Moving Toward the Post-Washington Consensus', *WIDER Annual Lectures*, 2, Helsinki: UNU/WIDER.

Stiglitz, Joseph (1999), 'Reforming the Global Financial Architecture: Lessons from Recent Crises', *Journal of Finance*, 54(4), 1508–22.

Stiglitz, Joseph (2000), 'What I Learned at the World Economic Crisis', *The New Republic*, 17 April.

Summers, Lawrence (1996a), 'Commentary', in Ricardo Hausmann and Liliana Rojas-Suarez (eds), *Volatile Capital Flows*, Washington, DC: Inter-American Development Bank.

Summers, Lawrence (1996b), 'Summers on Mexico: Ten Lessons to Learn', *The Economist*, 23 December, 52–4.

Summers, Lawrence (1998), 'Deputy Secretary Summers' Remarks Before the International Monetary Fund', Office of Public Affairs, US Treasury, *http:www.treas.gov/press/releases/pr2286.htm*.

Teik, Khoo Boo (1996), *Paradoxes of Mahathirism: An Intellectual Biography of Mahathir Mohamad*, Kuala Lumpur: Oxford University Press.

Tobin, James (1998), 'Asian financial crisis', *Japan and the World Economy*, 10: 351–3.

Tripathi, Salil, Ben Dolven and Faith Keenan (1998), 'Some Pains, Some Gains', *Far Eastern Economic Review*, 17 September, pp. 51–2.

UNCTAD (United Nations Conference on Trade and Development) (1998), *The Financial Crisis in Asia and Foreign Direct Investment: An Assessment*, Geneva: United Nations.

Wade, Robert (1998), 'From "miracle" to "cronyism": Explaining the great Asian slump', *Cambridge Journal of Economics*, 22: 693–706.

Warr, Peter G. (1986), 'Indonesia's other Dutch disease: Economic effects of the petroleum boom', in J.P. Neary and S. van Wijnbergen (eds), *Natural Resources and the Macroeconomy*, Oxford: Basil Blackwell, pp. 288–320.

Wei, Shang-Jin and Richard J. Zeckhauser (1998), 'Two crises and two Chinas', *Japan and the World Economy*, 10: 359–69.

Williamson, John (1993), 'A Cost Benefit Analysis of Capital Account Liberalisation', in Helmut Reisen and Bernhard Fischer (eds), *Financial Opening: Policy Issues and Experiences in Developing Countries*, Paris: OECD, pp. 25–34.

Williamson, John (1999), 'Development of the Financial System in Post-Crisis Asia', paper presented at the *High-Level Dialogue on Development Paradigms*, 10 December, Asian Development Bank Institute, Tokyo.

Williamson, John and Molly Mahar (1998), 'A Survey of Financial Liberalisation', *Essays in International Finance No. 211*, Princeton, NJ: International Finance section, Princeton University.

Wilson, Dominic (2000), 'Recent Developments in Asian Financial Markets', paper presented at the *Financial Markets and Policies in East Asia* conference, 4–5 September, Australian National University, Canberra.

World Bank (1993), *The East Asian Miracle: Economic Growth and Public Policy*, New York: Oxford University Press.

World Bank (1996), *Managing Capital Flows in East Asia*, Washington, DC: World Bank.

World Bank (1998), *Recovery in Asia*, Washington, DC: World Bank.

World Bank (2000), *East Asia: Recovery and Beyond*, Washington DC: World Bank.

Yap, Michael Meow-Chung (1999), 'Financial Crisis in Malaysia: Adjustment Through Unorthodox Policy', paper Presented in the Malaysia Forum, Department of Economics, Research School of Pacific and Asian Studies, 24 June, Australian National University, Canberra.

Yusof, Zainal Asman, Awang A. Hussain, Ismail Alowi, Lim Chee Sing and Sukhdave Singh (1994), 'Financial Reforms in Malaysia', in Gerard Caprio, Izak Atias and James A. Hanson (eds), *Financial Reform: Theory and Evidence*, Cambridge: Cambridge University Press, pp. 276–322.

Zefferys, Nicholas (1999), 'Doing Business in Malaysia: An American Ground Level Perspective' (a presentation by the author to foreign journalists visiting Malaysia in his capacity as the President of the American Malaysian Chamber of Commerce), *www.neac.gov.my*.

Index